Develop Your
NLP Skills

THE SUNDAY TIMES

C R E A T I N G   S U C C E S S

Develop Your
NLP Skills

Third edition

Andrew Bradbury

KOGAN
PAGE

London and Philadelphia

First edition published in 1997 as *NLP for Business Success*
Second edition published in 2000 as *Develop Your NLP Skills*
Third edition 2006
Reprinted 2006

120 Pentonville Road
London N1 9JN
United Kingdom
www.kogan-page.co.uk

525 South 4th Street, #241
Philadelphia PA 19147
USA

© Andrew J Bradbury, 1997, 2000, 2006

ISBN-10 0 7494 4558 0
ISBN-13 978 0 7494 4558 4

British Library Cataloguing in Publication Data

A CIP record for this book is available from the British Library.

Library of Congress Cataloging-in-Publication Data

Bradbury, Andrew (Andrew J.)
    Develop your NLP skills/Andrew Bradbury.–3rd ed.
        p.cm.–(Creating success series)
    ISBN 0-7494-4558-0
    1. Communication in management–Psychological aspects. 2. Neurolinguistic programming. 3. Self-actualization (Psychology) 4. Success in business I. Title: Develop your neurolinguistic programming skills. II. Title. III. Series: Creating success.
HD30.3.B687 2006
158.1–dc22
                                2006001616

Typeset by Jean Cussons Typesetting, Diss, Norfolk
Printed and bound in Great Britain by MPG Books Ltd, Bodmin, Cornwall

Contents

Thinking NLP

Taken as read

Whenever we interact with other people and/or with our environment, we do so on the basis of a whole multitude of presuppositions – assumptions about what is, or is not, true in a given situation.

In most cases these assumptions are based on prior experience of some kind. For example, when you get out of bed first thing in the morning, do you first look over the edge of the bed to check that there is a floor for you to stand on? Or do you simply take it for granted that the floor will be exactly where you left it the night before? And how time consuming would it be if you never made any assumptions but checked everything as though you had no prior experience to go on? (Sadly we know, from observing cases of Alzheimer's disease, how crippling this approach would be.)

So presuppositions are a very useful, even essential, part of everyday life. But even some of the presuppositions we most readily take for granted are not necessarily correct. Another common, but far less easily justified presupposition says that if you and I speak the same language then we will both attach the same meanings to the words we use. In reality, however, language is a comparatively unreliable resource, and we can quickly see the weakness of the assumption of shared meaning if we start trying to find universally agreed definitions for words like 'nice', 'beautiful', 'clever', 'justice' and 'education'. NLP – Neuro-Linguistic Programming – has its own underlying presuppositions. Depending on who you listen to, or read, there is now a fairly flexible list of anything up to about 25 different presuppositions, from which each NLP-oriented writer and training organisation has tended to select those entries which they believe express the most important aspects of NLP's core philosophy.

I have chosen those presuppositions which I believe are particularly relevant to the use of NLP in the business environment so that you can immediately get some idea of the thinking that underlies the techniques and methods you will be reading about in the rest of the book.

The presuppositions
Context makes meaning

We sometimes assume that things going on around us have a single, universal meaning. This presupposition proposes that 'meaning' is actually a mental construct (it exists in the mind of the perceiver, rather than in what is being perceived). And because meaning is linked to perception, it is determined by the context within which the perception occurs. When someone comes towards you holding a knife, it makes a real difference whether you are in your own kitchen and the person holding the knife is preparing food or whether it's in a dark alley and the person with the knife is demanding your money.

Every behaviour has a positive intention

This is possibly the most controversial of the NLP presuppositions, since it is so open to misinterpretation. What the presupposition means in the context of NLP is that every behaviour has a positive intention, *as far as the person exhibiting the behaviour is concerned.*

Can we really transpose such a *seemingly* idealistic concept to the business-place? George M Prince, writing in the *Harvard Business Review* some three years before the very first book on NLP was published, gives an excellent example of how this notion might be applied in management. He lists various 'contrasting assumptions' that make the difference between a negative, critical manager and a positive, supportive manager, including:

Judgmental Manager
When subordinates express themselves or act in ways unacceptable to me, I point out the flaws.

Judicious Manager
When subordinates express themselves or act in unacceptable ways, I assume they had reasons that made sense to them and explore the action from that point of view.

It is worth pointing out here that NLP does not claim that all behaviour is necessarily the best possible choice from an *objective* point of view. Nor does it suggest that all behaviour will have positive benefits for *everyone* involved.

Every behaviour is appropriate in some context

If we repeat a certain pattern of behaviour it is usually because once upon a time it produced a desired result. The trouble is that we often go on using some patterns even when, from an outsider's viewpoint, they are manifestly no longer appropriate. By implication, the most effective solution to unwanted behaviour is to find a more appropriate alternative rather than holding a lengthy, pointless post-mortem over the old behaviour (which is more likely to reinforce that old behaviour).

People will normally make the best choice available to them in any given situation

As well as having a positive intention, people will base their behaviour on *what seems to them* to be the best choice out of whatever choices they perceive as being available to them. At least two important influences are at work here.

Firstly, 'context makes meaning', but context itself is a matter of perception, and a person may perceive context A as being much like context B when, from an objective point of view, any similarities are purely superficial. Thus someone behaving inappropriately may simply have misunderstood the context.

Secondly, we have also seen that people will often repeat behaviour because it once worked, regardless of whether they see the past and present contexts as being similar.

In other words, no matter how calculating and rational we may try to be, making choices is a very subjective process, and what looks like a 'best' choice to one person may look like quite a poor choice to someone else.

The key issue is that few people ever deliberately, knowingly make a 'bad' choice.

A map is not the territory it depicts; words are not the things they describe; symbols are not the things they represent

'A map is not the territory' was originally coined by Alfred Korzybski (the founder of General Semantics):

> A map *is* not the territory it represents, but, if correct, it has a *similar structure* to the territory, which accounts for its usefulness.

(*Science and Sanity*, 5th edn, 1994, IGS, Englewood, NJ, p 58, italics as in the original)

In practical terms, this presupposition expresses the notion that we can never know everything there is to know about anything, no matter how simple. In order to make sense of the world around us, then, we 'draw' our own set of 'mental maps', but always on the basis of a selected subset of all possible information (just as a 'map' is not the landscape it depicts but merely a very limited subset of all possible information about that particular piece of the landscape).

People respond to their internal maps of reality, *not* to reality itself

At this point we can draw together the various concepts we've looked at so far and clear up a fairly widespread misunderstanding in the process. For the last 2,000 years and more, Western thinking has been in thrall to Aristotle's brand of two-valued thinking, which basically assumes that there is one right solution to every problem and everything else is wrong, that there is just one right view of any situation and every other view is wrong, and so on. This particular presupposition says that there are multiple possibilities in any problem (of varying degrees of utility), a variety of viewpoints in any situation, etc, because each person will have their own perceptions and in practice they will respond to those perceptions rather than to the objective reality that triggered those perceptions.

In contrast to Aristotelian thinking, this NLP concept of 'personal perception' is closer to the solipsistic teaching that predominated before Socrates, Plato and Aristotle started to rock the philosophical boat. There are, however, at least two varieties of solipsism, rather than just one, namely *epistemological* solipsism and *metaphysical* solipsism.

Epistemological solipsism, which is the viewpoint NLP is based upon, does not deny the existence of an external, 'absolute' reality; it simply says that each of us has an internal representation of that reality, which is what we base our thoughts and behaviour on. Metaphysical solipsism, which some writers have (wrongly) assumed NLP supports, holds that there is *no* external reality and that therefore everything is just a fantasy playing out in someone's mind. Just whose mind that might be is anybody's guess.

As one of Bob Dylan's lyrics has it, 'I'll let you be in my dream, if you'll let me be in yours.'

If you go on doing what you're doing now you are very likely to go on getting the same results as you are getting now

This is the first part of an optimistic presupposition, which emphasises the fact that, in *any* situation, we always have choices.

Though we may not be able to control what goes on in the world around us, we can *always* control how we *respond* to those events. If we always act/respond in the same way then the most likely result is that we will maintain the status quo.

If you want something different you must do something different, and keep varying your behaviour until you get the result that you want

The second part of the presupposition is that there are solutions to every situation if you're prepared to keeping on looking until you find them.

In a business context this points us to the fact that if change is required, then it had better be genuine change, not just an exercise in 'skilled incompetence', as Chris Argyris calls it – adopting new processes, but using old methods to carry them out (like trying to play a CD on a gramophone).

The person with the greatest number of choices in a given situation is most likely to achieve their outcome

Building on the previous presupposition, from an NLP viewpoint developing multiple options in any situation is seen as being more realistic than having only one or two. Indeed, from an NLP perspective:

■ One option is no choice at all.
■ Two options is a dilemma.
■ Real choice only starts when you have at *least* three options.

Change makes change

It is a common saying that 'the only person you can really change is yourself'. NLP goes one step further and also acknowledges that changing your own behaviour inevitably has an effect on the people around you. The underlying notion, derived from cybernetics, is that when one element within a system changes, the whole system must change in order to adapt to that changed element. That 'system' may be your family and/or your friends and/or the people you work with, and so on, depending on what it is you decide to change.

You cannot *not* communicate

This presupposition simply makes the point that we are constantly communicating, both by what we do *and* by what we don't do, by what we say *and* by what we don't say, by the messages we send deliberately *and* by a host of mainly unconscious non-verbal signals.

Thus it is clearly in our own interest to understand the communication process as far as we can and to learn how to become effective communicators rather than simply leaving things to chance.

The meaning of your communication is the response that you get

The presupposition here is that people can only respond to what they *think* you mean, which may, or may not, be an accurate interpretation of your *intended* meaning.

(Please note: in this context, a 'communication' is the 'whole' message – not only what you *said* but also all of the accompanying non-verbal signals.)

What this presupposition explains is that, if we want people to respond appropriately to what we say, then we need to talk *to* them rather than *at* them. That is, we need to be constantly aware of other people's responses to what we're saying, and adjust our communication accordingly, rather than just assuming that they will have understood what we meant them to understand.

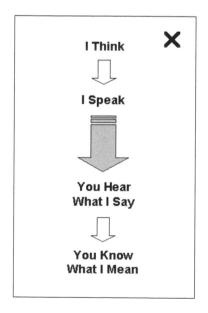

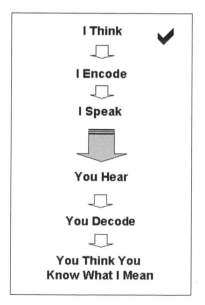

This presupposition does admittedly cause a certain amount of confusion on occasion. Quite a few people seem to think that it also means: 'Whatever I *think* your communication means must be what you *intended* it to mean.' This is an unjustified assumption and makes for poor communication.

Effective communication requires active participation on *both* sides. On the one hand it is certainly the responsibility of the person sending a message to check whether the message has been received and understood correctly, and to provide appropriate clarification if it hasn't. And it is the responsibility of the recipients of a message to indicate what clarification they need, if any, and to accept that clarification, even if it indicates a different meaning from the one in their initial interpretation.

Everyone has all of the resources they need

What this means is simply that a person is ultimately able to deal with any situation in which they may find themselves by drawing on their own inner resources (or capabilities), or by developing new resources, rather than by relying on someone or something else to give them a resource that they didn't previously have.

Having said that, according to *Bradbury's corollaries*, in order to use a resource you must:

■ know that you have it;
■ know how to use it (though not necessarily at a *conscious* level).

Genuine understanding only comes with experience

Whilst we can gain knowledge by a variety of routes – reading, talking, watching other people and so on – nothing is so completely educational, in a positive sense, as experience. You don't really *understand* something until you've done it yourself.

There is no such thing as failure, only feedback

When something doesn't go as we planned we often tend to see that as *failure*. Depending on the seriousness of the situation we might then get angry, irritated, sad, depressed, worried, guilty or whatever. None of which serves any useful purpose.

But what if we see the situation as *feedback* rather than *failure* – a demonstration of how *not* to do something? Instead of being wrong, we've learnt something. Instead of feeling bad, we are free to form a new plan of action and try again.

There is a story about a certain investment banker, one of whose assistants made a business decision that cost the company millions of dollars. When the assistant was called to the banker's office he expected to get a thorough roasting and quite possibly an invitation to seek new career opportunities – somewhere else.

'I'm so sorry, sir,' the young man exclaimed, as soon as he entered the banker's office. 'I wouldn't blame you one little bit if you fired me on the spot!'

'Fire you?' the banker answered, 'when it's cost the company several million dollars to train you in the finer points of risk management? Not a chance. I only called you in to make sure you'd learnt the lesson.'

Your brain and your body are indivisible parts of the same system

The notion that our body and our brain are separate entities seems to have developed within the medical profession in the 1930s and 1940s. If there was something wrong with the body – from a sniffle to malignant cancer – the only solution was some kind of physical treatment. And despite its position at the *head* of the central nervous system, in mainstream medicine it was received wisdom that the influence of the brain effectively stopped at the neck.

At the very same time, however, Alfred Korzybski and the General Semanticists were investigating the idea that mental activity had a direct correlation to physiological activity.

Only in the last couple of decades has practical, scientifically verifiable evidence come to light that shows beyond reasonable doubt that the immune system, for example, is integrally linked to brain activity, so that mental stress can inhibit the performance of the immune system and thus lead to a lowering of general physical health.

People aren't 'broken' and don't need to be 'fixed'

The old psychiatric metaphor put seemingly inappropriate communications and/or behaviour on a par with a broken arm or leg. This led to the assumption that people could be mentally 'broken' and 'fixed' just as they could be physically broken and fixed. According to NLP, however, this is an inappropriate and misleading metaphor. W Edwards Deming ('father' of the Japanese industrial revolution) seems to have had a similar idea in mind when he offered this advice: 'If people don't get it, don't fix the people – fix the process.'

Checkpoint action

Pause from time to time in your everyday activities and notice what presuppositions you believe in.

For example, do you think that people are basically OK – trustworthy and capable of being loyal and responsible, even though they may need a little guidance from time to time? Or do you see people as being basically self-centred and untrustworthy and therefore in need of regular monitoring to ensure that they don't get up to something they shouldn't?

2

Introducing NLP

Ahead of its time

NLP – Neuro-Linguistic Programming – is one of the most powerful tools currently available to the business community. The term 'neuro-linguistic' was coined by Alfred Korzybski several decades ago, but NLP – developed by Richard Bandler, John Grinder *et al* – has gone far beyond Korzybski's original ideas to become a synthesis of many of the most effective psychological techniques around.

In January 2005, for instance, an article in *New Scientist* magazine entitled 'Doors of Perception' tackled the case for arguing that we actually have at least 21 senses rather than just five, and that 'the senses are less than primary, and that perception is what we really get'. NLP has taken a similar viewpoint for two decades or more, with its emphasis on modalities (the standard five senses) *and* sub-modalities, the constituent parts of the main senses such as (for vision) colour or black and white, stills (like photographs) or motion (like a video or a film), and so on. Moreover, NLP's interest in the sub-modalities specifically addresses the way in which changes in these individual elements can alter someone's overall perception.

For example, think of a recent, pleasurable experience, something of no great importance. Depending on how you tend to remember things – mainly in pictures, or sounds, or feelings

– or any combination thereof – notice, in the case of a visual image, whether the image is brightly coloured or is in softer tones, or maybe in black, white and shades of grey. Is the picture moving or still? Is it in sharp focus, soft focus or maybe a little blurred?

If your image is based around sounds, what are you hearing – are there voices, music, street noises or the sounds of the countryside, etc? Are the noises clear or muffled? Where are they coming from and are they in stereo or mono?

And if your image is mainly about feelings – emotional and/or tactile – what *are* you feeling? Are textures involved, and if so are they rough or smooth? Do you feel warm or cool, or even cold? Does the image involve feeling relaxed or alert?

Now, whatever you answered to those questions, keep thinking of that experience and start changing the qualities of your image. For example, if you 'saw' bright colours, tone them down. If you heard soft noises, make them louder. If you felt relaxed, imagine yourself becoming tensed up.

Do this with each of the qualities of your image, and notice how it alters your experience.

What's in a name?

The name *Neuro-Linguistic Programming* breaks down into:

▪ *Neuro –*	which covers what goes on in the brain and in the nervous system.
▪ *Linguistic –*	referring to the way that we use words, and how this affects our perceptions of, and relationship with, the external world.
▪ *Programming –*	an interactive process which allows us to make very precise choices about the way we think, speak and feel. The exercise on submodalities is a typical example of what we mean by 'programming'.

It could be said that standard management theory tends to be a bit like the scientist who discovered that bees 'cannot' fly (their wings are too small, their bodies are an aerodynamic nightmare, and so on). Likewise, there are plenty of ideas about 'what's' wrong with management, but not many on 'how' to change things for the better.

NLP, on the other hand, is like the experienced beekeeper who ignores the scientific view and goes on helping his bees to be as productive as possible.

In other words, NLP deals with things the way they *are* rather than getting bogged down in what *ought to be*. It offers an in-depth understanding of what really happens when we communicate, and the means to use that knowledge so as to maximise the effectiveness of any interpersonal transaction, be it sales, negotiation, a presentation, an appraisal or whatever.

WIIFM – what's in it for me?

Any business person who has a grasp of the basic NLP concepts and techniques, and who learns how to utilise this information effectively, can expect to enjoy a significant improvement in all aspects of their business *and* social activities.

In practical terms, NLP can help you to become more successful in business by:

■ setting effective goals and planning better, leading to more focused action;
■ building good-quality relationships with colleagues and business associates, replacing conflict with co-operation;
■ developing greater flexibility in the way that you respond to your environment, leading to more appropriate responses to the ever-changing demands of your business;
■ managing your mental activities, leading to greater self-control and more effective self-management.

One of the core skills in NLP is the process of 'modelling' successful people in all walks of life (as judged by their peers). Having modelled various aspects of a person's behaviour and thinking (see Chapter 19), it is then possible to compare the results with those of their less successful colleagues in order to spot the 'differences that make the difference'. This is the 'how' of: find out what works, then do it.

By implication, this means that the techniques described in NLP are all based on what some people are already doing. You may already be using some of these skills yourself without even recognising them for what they are. It is this lack of awareness that locks us into the predicament where what leads to success in one situation can lead to failure in another.

> We already have all the resources we need to deal with almost any situation in which we may find ourselves.

Influencing with integrity

Because they are rooted in proven success, these ideas and techniques are extremely powerful, and it may seem that there is a very real chance that they can be misused.

Quite right. Just as you can use a hammer to build a beautiful boat, or hit your thumb, or bash somebody's head in, these techniques can be used for good or ill. But as Genie Laborde points out, in her book *Influencing with Integrity*, there are clear consequences attached to using NLP in a manipulative manner:

■ Resentment;
■ Recrimination;
■ Remorse;
■ Revenge.

Using this book

The purpose of this book is to provide a *practical* guide to using NLP to achieve business excellence. As far as the layout is concerned, rather than repeat the same piece of information several times over, the basic details of the various NLP techniques and ideas are set out in Chapters 1–16. Chapters 17–24 describe how NLP can be applied in various business situations and when necessary refer back to the chapter where a technique was first described. For example, wherever a *meta program* is referred to in Chapters 17–24 (in the chapter on meetings, for instance) the reader is simply referred back to Chapter 12.

Chapters 1–16 either include exercises or end with one or more *checkpoint actions* which will help you to build on the points covered in that chapter. This allows us to present the information in a succinct manner that underlines in a practical way the highly integrated nature of NLP theory and practice.

Developing NLP skills

As you read through this book you will discover that it is very easy to pick up the basic ideas in NLP. Becoming proficient in the use of NLP techniques takes just a little bit longer. This process can be thought of as four levels of competence:

1. **Unconscious incompetence:** You don't know what you don't know.
2. **Conscious incompetence:** You are very aware of what you don't know.
3. **Conscious competence:** You are very aware of what you do know.
4. **Unconscious competence:** You can use your knowledge without having to think about it.

Let me illustrate the four levels by introducing you to an important NLP skill known as 'sensory acuity'.

Level 1

Many readers may respond to that last sentence by asking what is meant by the term 'sensory acuity'. In other words, on this particular topic they are at Level 1, 'unconscious incompetence'.

In a business context, recognising when you are at Level 1 on a given subject and acting accordingly are valuable skills in their own right.

Level 2

I now explain that the mind and the body are both parts of a single system. I go on to say that sensory acuity is the process of observing another person's physiological responses – changes in skin colour and in muscular tension and relaxation, etc – and that this gives you some insight into that person's mental activity. You might then think of people blushing because they are embarrassed, or clenching their jaw muscles because they are angry or frustrated. You have begun to understand what sensory acuity is about, though you are still only aware of the most obvious examples of the body–brain connection.

You have moved up a level, but NLP may still *appear* to be no more than a set of tricks and techniques.

Level 3

After a time, whilst you still need to practise your skills, you will be able to spot the more subtle physical signals, when you remember to think about them.

Again you have moved up a level, and you will have begun to understand that there is far more to NLP than meets the eye.

Level 4

Finally, with practice, experience, and preferably with some professional tutoring, you will be able to respond to other people's behaviour in a highly effective, yet effortless manner.

You have reached Level 4: 'unconscious competence', where you can use your NLP skills to full effect as a natural and instinctive reaction to whatever situation you find yourself in.

The choice is yours

In place of a checkpoint action for this chapter, I want to demonstrate the point I made earlier: Everyone has the resources they need to cope with any situation.

How often have you heard someone say something like: 'He (or she) makes me so angry'? Probably too often to keep count, yet this is actually a completely false assessment of how other people's behaviour can affect us. After all, if it were really possible for another person to *make* me angry then that person must have greater control over my emotions than I do. In practice, our emotional reactions to the events around us are actually based on our *perceptions* of those events, and our perceptions, as we will see in just a moment, are entirely under our own control.

As a very simple example of selective perception, the verb 'To speak one's mind' might be conjugated thus:

I believe in being frank
You are outspoken
He is downright rude

On a more serious note, if I am in control of my emotions, then even under the most trying conditions, I am free to decide whether I will control the situation – or simply react. In order to make a choice I must *know* what resources I have available to me, which is what this demonstration is about.

When you do this exercise you should read each step – *and carry out the required action* – before moving on to the next step.

Step 1

Think of a situation at work which, whilst not too serious, has caused you a certain degree of annoyance or irritation.

Recall the event as though you were watching a film (close your eyes if it helps). Watch the film, listen to the soundtrack – people talking and so on – and recall any feelings, both physical and emotional, which are part of the event. Watch the whole film before going on to **Step 2**.

Step 2

Stand up and briefly shake each arm and each leg. (In NLP this is known as *breaking state*.) Then think of a piece of music which you like and which is completely opposite in mood to the event you recalled in **Step 1**. If several different pieces of music suggest themselves, select one piece in particular before moving to **Step 3**.

Step 3

Now run that film again, but this time include, as part of the soundtrack, the piece of music you selected in **Step 2**.

Run the whole film before reading **Step 4**.

Step 4

Finally, break state (see **Step 2**) and then run the film through one more time, *without* the music. Notice how your emotional feelings have changed – how the negative sensations have lessened, or even disappeared.

You have just experienced more first-hand evidence of how your perceptions shape your feelings, and how you can control or, in NLP terms, *program* your perceptions, and thus your feelings, to produce a positive and beneficial state of mind.

You have always had this resource, and may have used it many times (playing a favourite record to remind you of a special occasion, for example), without consciously understanding the process involved. Now you both have the resource *and* know how to use it.

The rest of this book will show how various NLP techniques can be used to make you more positive and effective in every area of your business activities. You may also find various ways to use them to improve other parts of your life as well.

3

Points of view

The map is not the territory

Our ability to interact with the external world is greatly influenced by our very restricted *conscious* abilities. For example, whilst we receive an estimated 2.4 million *bits* of information every minute (through our various senses), we can only consciously handle about 300–500 bits of information per minute grouped in 7 ± 2 *chunks*. The remaining 2.35 million bits of information are dealt with at the *un*conscious level.

This process of abstracting a limited picture of the total reality in which we live is referred to in NLP as mapping or map-making. Not surprisingly, given such a mass of information, no two people ever have *exactly* the same map of any part of the external world. On the contrary, a single word can be the basis for two quite separate maps:

(Please note that the terms 'maps' and 'map-making' are used throughout this chapter to refer to *mental* maps and the way we verbally describe them.)

Everyone has their own personal views of the world, their own 'maps of reality'. Even in this book there are certain things that will not tally with the experiences of every single reader.

Neuroscientist Professor Walter J Freeman gives an admirably succinct description of the basic map-making process in his book *How Brains Make Up Their Minds* (1999, Phoenix, London):

> ...the brain responds to the world by destabilizing the primary sensory cortices of the brain. The result is the construction of neural activity patterns, which provide the elements of which meaning is made. When the freshly made patterns are transmitted to other parts of the brain, the raw sense data that triggered them are washed away. What remains is what has been made within the brain.

So, whilst we need to create these maps in order to make some sense of the world around us, we must also be aware that even the best map is only a very rough guide to the landscape it represents:

A Word		The THING it describes
A Map	**IS NOT**	The PLACE it depicts
A Symbol		The THING it represents

One very important way of making our communications more effective (and our relationships more harmonious) is by being aware of both the strengths *and the limitations* of our mental maps. An essential part of becoming a mature person lies in recognising, and learning to live with, the vital difference between 'this is true/not true' and 'this is true/not true *for me*'.

At the end of Jane's presentation Bob criticised the way that she had used bullet points on some of her slides and numbering in the handout. 'If you use numbers in the notes then you *must* use numbers on your slides,' he insisted. 'That's the proper way of conducting a lecture.'

Bob had clearly understood the relationship between the numbered notes and the bulleted slides, so it wasn't the numbering and bullet points as *such* that had caused the upset. The 'real problem' was that Jane's style was at odds with Bob's internal map of how a 'lecture' should be presented. Bob overlooked the fact that there were 30 people at the presentation, each of whom may also have had a view of what constituted a 'good presentation'. Yet all of the other 29 people chose to ignore any reservations they might have had in order to get the most out of the presentation.

So Bob had a point about the inconsistency, but in practical terms he created an element of conflict, and reduced his own ability to find the presentation useful, enjoyable or informative, by insisting that his map alone was valid.

In practice, our knowledge, on any subject you care to name, will *always* be incomplete. Likewise, no matter how much care and thought we give it, we can never be totally accurate in our description of any person, thing, event or whatever. As one writer put it:

■ Whatever we do or say, it is certain that we will be misunderstood – to some degree.

■ Whatever we see or hear, it is certain we will misunderstand it – to some degree.

■ We can never eliminate misunderstandings – but this should not deter us from striving to *minimise* them.

Sometimes this can be difficult, especially when it seems as though you're the only person willing to make the effort.

If maps were real we'd all be somewhere else!

We start constructing mental maps more or less from the day we are born. It's how we store our life experience. Yet, as we grow into adulthood, some people make as few new maps as they can by filtering incoming information to such an extent that almost everything is forced to conform to their existing perceptions. Some people pretend to make fresh maps, though they are mainly only transcribing their existing maps. And some people make new maps all through their lives, both for the fun of it and because they regularly seek out new experiences to learn from.

There are at least three major reasons why a regular supply of new maps is desirable:

1. Maps are *always* based on a limited view of *external* reality, which is itself in a constant process of change.
2. The longer we use any particular map, the harder it becomes to recognise its shortcomings.
3. The more familiar a map becomes, the harder it is to accept the validity of anybody else's map of the same 'territory'.

Since every map is necessarily incomplete, whenever we create a new map we are forced to be selective about the information we include, a result usually arrived at by evaluating current information in the light of maps we have already prepared.

This opens the door to three more ways of misunderstanding external reality:

1. **Generalisation:** Assuming that a rule which applies to a specific situation will be equally appropriate everywhere else.
2. **Distortion:** Editing our perceptions to create a more acceptable version of reality.
3. **Deletion:** Ignoring information we don't like or can't be bothered with.

Some typical (misleading) workplace maps include:

■ 'A tidy desk shows a tidy mind.'
   (Does a clear desk show an empty mind?)
■ 'We expect our staff to behave in a professional manner.'
   (Going by the dictionary definition that simply means 'we
   expect that our staff will only work if they get paid for it'.)
■ 'Customers don't want to be bothered with...'
   (Who says so? Where and what is the evidence? Did anyone
   bother to ask the customers?)

Checkpoint action

Listen to the conversations around you with the following thoughts
in mind:

   a. Are any generalisations, distortions or deletions being
      used?
   b. What assumptions does each person seem to be making?
   c. Are those assumptions justified?
   d. What do these assumptions tell you about the speaker's
      mental maps?
   e. What could you say to each speaker which would help
      them to get a better understanding of other people's points
      of view?

4

Cultures, values and beliefs

Company map or virtual reality?

Strange but true, three of the most basic elements of company life – the company vision, the company mission and even company culture – are actually maps. What is more, calling them a 'company' vision and a 'company' mission is often highly misleading.

Unfortunately many companies devise mission statements that are decidedly short on content, as can be seen in the example below, which appeared in a brochure put out by a major academic examination board:

> To facilitate the best methods of flexible and effective supervisory and management education, development and assessment.

It sounds terrific, but what does it mean?

Does any reputable company deliberately set out to use *second* best methods? And what exactly do they mean by 'best', 'flexible' and 'effective' – all highly subjective words?

'Best' compared with what? How 'flexible'? Who defined their methods as 'effective', and what yardstick was used?

As an indicator of the company's intentions this statement is essentially a meaningless collection of buzzwords. As a 'map' it depicts a 'territory' that is little more than virtual reality.

All for one and...?

We need to recognise that a business map only has value if it embodies a *shared* reality. According to Alan Harrison at the School of Business Management, Brunel University: 'Behind the often bland facade of corporate communications, the language used encodes internal conflict and contradictions.' A survey by researchers at Brunel University showed that staff are beginning to decode company circulars and are turning against their employers as a result. 'They are particularly dismissive of the use of "we" to imply shared objectives,' says Harrison.

As another business commentator observed:

> If your company mission has to be written down and passed around, you don't have a *company* mission.

Companies which ignore this message and rely on imposed maps will, of necessity, have a punitive, autocratic culture which leaves little room for individuality. They may flourish for a while, but sooner or later they begin to crumble. The process may not become terminal if the management style can be changed in time – by re-educating the existing management or by a major reorganisation. But the changes must be genuine, or the reorganisation itself may simply speed the collapse.

As a point of interest, I originally wrote that last paragraph both as a generalisation and with a specific company in mind. Not long after the second edition of this book came out, the company I was thinking of underwent the kind of major change that I described, including the removal of certain senior managers, and has now been taken back into the parent organisation.

No matter what the style may be, company culture is usually

set by senior management, and tends to change almost imperceptibly unless there is a major upheaval at that level.

In NLP, great emphasis is placed on the need to remain true to your personal values and beliefs (see Chapter 16). If your working life seems unduly stressful, a worthwhile first step towards resolving the situation can be to review your own life maps, particularly your values and beliefs, in relation to your company's culture. On the one hand a gradual drift into a new culture may have created a situation where you no longer share the prevailing value-set. Alternatively, the actual day-to-day running of the company may be at odds with its declared mission and vision. In either case it may be that the simple act of identifying the mismatch is sufficient to ease the stress.

A certain American banking company sold its UK-based software house to a British company which had frequent dealings with the military establishment. Within a year 10 of the top technicians, who were one of the reasons why the British company had been keen to acquire this particular software house, had moved to companies where they would not be required to work on projects related to the defence industry.

A matter of choice

In that last example, the employees saw their situation as being *two-valued* – either/or. In most cases, however, it is more useful to view a situation from *multiple* standpoints, each of which offers its own choice(s). Remember, it is a basic tenet of NLP that you don't really have a choice at all until you have at least *three* separate options to hand. Indeed, seasoned practitioners of NLP won't even bother to count how many options they have, since the most effective response is one which changes even as the situation changes.

But what happens if you find that your personal values are at odds with those of your employer? Do you really have to hand in your resignation, or put your personal beliefs to one side while you are at work? Not at all. Just one of the alternatives is to work for promotion, in the company or in your union (if you belong to one), so as to have a greater input on company policy.

If you go on doing what you're doing now, you'll go on getting what you're getting now.

If you *want* something different, you have to change what you are *doing* until you get what you want.

There is a popular business model often referred to as 'circles of influence', according to which there are two areas of influence – the area in which you can exert influence over what is going on, and everywhere else (where you have no influence). If we adopt this model we should never try to act outside our area of influence, because we will simply be wasting our time and energy. The trouble is, to paraphrase George Bernard Shaw:

> The reasonable man adapts himself to his circle of influence;
> The unreasonable one persists in trying to expand his circle of influence.
> Therefore all progress depends on the unreasonable man.

NLP goal setting (which will be covered in more detail in Chapter 6) tends to favour a more flexible view, based on what is influenceable, what is ecological and what is strategic:

▨ **Influenceable:** Notice that we're talking about what is 'influenceable', in a general sense, rather than what can be influenced by a particular person. In line with NLP's focus on increasing choices, this is based on the perception that we do not know how far our influence can extend until we've tried it out.

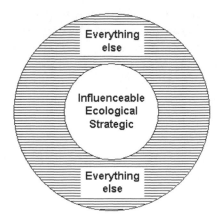

■ **Ecological:** Only take time to exert influence where it will serve a useful purpose. Sometimes we can get so irritated or frustrated by a situation that, even though we know that it is really rather trivial or irrelevant or will take an undue amount of time and effort to resolve, we get involved anyway. That is an *un*ecological approach.

■ **Strategic:** Using your influence to get results today is fairly pointless if this approach generates more and/or bigger problems in the future. Use influence where, so far as you can tell, it will bring strategic (lasting) benefits – or start building a pigeon loft right now for when the birds come home to roost.

The pursuit of excellence

Nothing ever stays the same, and no business, large or small, can ever afford to rest on its laurels. So, in a business context, the old saying 'If it ain't broke, don't fix it' isn't always the best policy. Of course there is no point in adopting change for its own sake, but any company that wants to stay ahead of the game must be constantly checking its maps against the external situation, and making appropriate adjustments when necessary.

Moreover, the process of change must be customised for each company. Beware the consultant who offers stock solutions to all of their clients. Some time ago certain 'experts' espoused Japanese work styles, but it soon turned out to be an approach that produced strictly limited success. To be of practical use, a business map must take account of local customs, culture, social parameters, and especially of changing customer needs and expectations. That which is true for Osaka is not necessarily true for Tokyo, let alone for Detroit, Manchester or Hamburg. Trying to make a company fit a particular business theory is like altering the landscape to fit a map. Generic business theories are fine, as long as they are recognised as such and are applied at the right level. There is a point at which the application of unmodified ideas automatically becomes counterproductive.

Checkpoint actions

1. To what extent does the management in your company act in accordance with the declared mission/vision?
2. As briefly as possible, how would you describe the culture in each of the companies you have worked for in the past?
3. From the list you drew up for question 2, what was particularly good or bad about each culture?
4. Using the assessments you made in question 3, what could you do to improve, or encourage improvement in, the culture of your present company?
5. List the three beliefs and three values which are most important in your life. Then discuss your selection with someone whose judgement you trust.

5

The medium is the message

Representational systems

In the last chapter we talked briefly about creating mental maps, and how these maps are likely to vary from person to person, even when they apparently relate to the same event. One reason why this happens is because of the way we use what NLP calls *representational systems*, or just *rep systems*.

There are five of these rep systems, because they are directly related to our five main senses: sight, hearing, feeling, taste and smell. They are called representational systems, or PTSs (Preferred Thinking Styles), simply because these are the five ways in which we process and store incoming information, or how we represent the external world to ourselves. And as a result these are the five elements of any memory to which we pay most attention. (In this context a 'memory' refers to any information stored in our brain.)

For those people who have all five senses in good working order it may seem like common sense to suppose that, since we use all of our senses all the time that we are awake, we therefore tend to give more or less equal weight to information coming through all five 'channels'. And yet most of the time that's exactly what we don't do. In order to reduce the flood of incoming information to a manageable stream we ignore large amounts of that information – at a conscious level. That is to say, we tend to give more attention to information arriving via one or two *preferred* channels and ignore much of what comes in via the other senses.

(Various studies appear to support the view that, even though we are consciously aware of only a limited amount of what is going on around us, we take in and store a far larger amount of information on a sub- or out-of-conscious level.)

Prior to Bandler and Grinder's collaboration, psychologists had been aware of the basic facts that I've just mentioned – but without really understanding how the pieces all fitted together. What Bandler and Grinder noticed was that we don't just use the five senses to sort information, we also tend to move our eyes to different positions and selectively use certain words, called predicates, in ways that indicate which sense or senses are uppermost in our thinking processes at any moment:

Visual mode

The three visual eye positions, or *eye accessing cues*, as seen from an observer's point of view, are:

Visual imagine   Visualisation   Visual recall

A predicate, in the NLP context, is a word that predicates, or implies, a particular sensory system. Visual predicates include:

'I *see* what you mean.'
'*Look*s good to me.'
'*Show* me more.'

Auditory mode

Auditory mode also has three eye positions (as seen by an observer):

Auditory imagine   Internal dialogue   Auditory recall

And its own set of predicates, such as:

'I *hear* what you say.'
'*Sounds* good to me.'
'*Tell* me more.'

Kinaesthetic mode

Although kinaesthetic mode can be particularly powerful, only one eye position has been found to fit this mode:

Kinaesthetic recall

This is partly due to the belief that feelings cannot be constructed or imagined without actually re-experiencing some source event – be it emotional or tactile – in the same way that you could create a visual or auditory fantasy, such as a croco-dile riding a bicycle, or your boss talking like Bugs Bunny. Thus kinaesthetic mode is always about *recalled* experience. Kinaesthetic predicates would include:

'I *get* what you're saying.'
'I *feel* good about that.'
'*Fill me in* on the details.'

The whole area of sensory predicates is all the more influential because we are usually wholly unaware that this filtering process is taking place. When a conversation between two people is based on different PTSs they are likely to find effective communication very difficult without knowing why, to the point where they might as well be talking different languages. 'I just couldn't seem to get through to him/her.'

Each can hear what the other person is *saying*, yet they find it almost impossible to understand what the other person *means*.

When PTSs collide:

Jim: Have you looked at those papers I showed you?
Ann: I'm afraid I was tied up with other business all day.
Jim: You mean you didn't even glance at them?
Ann: You didn't tell me they had to be dealt with in a hurry.
Jim: Well they do! Now, when am I going to see some action?

A 'shared view':

Sue: Have you looked at those papers I showed you?
Tom: Not yet. You must have seen how busy I've been today.
Sue: So you haven't had a chance to glance through them?
Tom: No I haven't – but now that my desk is clear I'll give them my full attention.
Sue: That's great! When can I expect to see your report on my desk?

What's in a mode?

It is important to understand that the various sensory 'modes' or representational systems are aspects of our behaviour. They are definitely *not* 'who we are'. So whilst it is tempting to talk about 'visuals', 'auditories', etc, this can easily lead us into thinking that people have just one or two preferred thinking styles which they use all of the time. This in turn leads to the assumption that once you know a person's preferred thinking style you can use that same style whenever you need to communicate with them, and you are guaranteed to be in tune with the way they register what is going on in the world.

In practice people switch between rep systems quite frequently (some more frequently than others), and for a variety of reasons. This was particularly evident in a TV series that ran in the UK a few years ago. Each programme featured three amateur chefs who would be shown preparing a three-course meal, of their own devising, which would be judged by a well-known professional chef, a celebrity of some description and the show's presenter. An interesting aspect of the behaviour of the professional chefs was that, almost without exception, whilst the meals were being prepared most of their comments were about how the food smelt. Once the meals were complete and ready for judging, however, the chefs changed from using olfactory predicates to visual and gustatory predicates to describe the food.

Checkpoint action

Listen out for rep system predicates in the way people, including yourself, describe the world around them. How does this help you to understand the way people are currently perceiving their situation?

6

Know what you want to get what you want

What do you *really* really want?

The results we get in life are largely self-generated. That is to say, we tend to notice the things that confirm our current expectations. In order to succeed you must assume and believe that you are going to succeed. But this goes deeper than mere 'positive thinking'.

> Whether you think you will succeed or you think you will fail, it is almost certain that you will be proved correct.

But how will you recognise success? Positive thinking, though infinitely preferable to negative thinking, is a fairly hit and miss way of achieving a desired result. Motivational speakers and pep rallies actually have a strictly limited, short-term effect. Take this example of a sales director intending to inspire his 'troops':

> You are the greatest sales team it has ever been my privilege to lead. In the coming year we must be leaner and fitter, make more sales and maximise our profitability. The recent downturn may be over but we aren't out of the woods yet.
> We *can* do it. I *believe* we can do it. I *know* we can do it!

Like the mission statement in the last chapter, the rhetoric is stirring indeed, but what does it really mean? What is the measure of 'leaner and fitter'? How many extra sales equal 'more'? Does this mean that the sales people will no longer be able to offer ad hoc discounts to special customers, for example?

Maybe the sales director has just discovered Pareto's Law (and assumes that just 20 per cent of the company's customers will account for approximately 80 per cent of its sales)? If so, does he want the sales team to 'maximise profitability' by ignoring the less profitable 80 per cent of their customer base?

The audience may give the sales director a standing ovation as he finishes his speech, but will anyone actually improve their performance as a result of this purely emotive appeal?

Almost certainly 'no', mainly because there are no clear outcomes to which the sales people can respond.

The power of a well-formed outcome

Defining outcomes is a process of self-empowerment.

If I have a well-formed (clearly defined) outcome, I can make effective decisions about what I am prepared to do in order to achieve that outcome. I will also be able to assess whether, at any stage, my outcome has become impractical and must be adapted or abandoned.

Without a well-formed outcome I have little choice but to simply react to what is going on around me. Without a clear sense of direction, regardless of my status, I will be relatively ineffectual. As a result, I am likely to become increasingly frustrated, resentful and even vindictive.

People respond to and work well for a person who obviously knows what he is doing, and who is able to communicate positively and effectively with his superiors, colleagues and subordinates. How are you going to convince anyone that you know what you are doing, let alone encourage them to follow your lead, if your outcome(s) aren't clear in your own mind?

> Your perceptions and thoughts are interactive, therefore your current outcome will help to decide which external and internal signals you are consciously aware of.

Look, listen or feel

In order to configure effective outcomes we first need to understand the concept of *Preferred Thinking Styles* (PTSs) – the ways in which we mentally represent the external world inside our heads. The three most frequently used styles are: visual, auditory and kinaesthetic – in *pictures*, by *sounds* or through *feelings* (both physical and emotional).

These PTSs tend to be related to the culture in which a person lives. In the USA, for example, the prevailing culture is highly visual, and over 50 per cent of the population have this as their PTS. In France, however, both the culture and the dominant PTS are auditory. The UK is somewhere in between, but seems to be moving towards a primarily visual culture.

People will often give verbal and non-verbal signals which indicate which PTS(s) they are currently using. One type of non-verbal signal can be seen in people's eye movements (see Chapter 5), while the most readily recognisable verbal signal is found in the specific words chosen to convey a particular idea. The three statements below all say the same thing, but each uses a markedly different choice of words:

▨ *Visual:* 'I don't *see* what all the fuss is about – it *looks* pretty straightforward to me.'

▨ *Auditory:* 'It *sounds* like a lot of fuss about nothing if you *ask* me. I'd *say* it was pretty straightforward.'

▨ *Kinaesthetic:* 'I don't know what people are *getting* so *upset* about. I *found* it pretty straightforward.'

Using language which reflects the other person's PTS is a key element in effective communication. If, in a conversation, you spot that the other person is using mainly *kinaesthetic* words and phrases, and you discreetly match their phraseology, you are creating an implied link between that person and yourself. If, however, you keep using *visual* phraseology to a person whose own phraseology clearly says that they are in *auditory* or *kinaesthetic* mode, then you mustn't be surprised if agreement is hard to come by.

What does success look, sound and feel like?

Because each individual gives somewhat different weighting to the three PTSs, and may favour different PTSs in different situations, we need to take account of all three sensory modes when setting our goals in order to create an outcome which is personally meaningful.

For example, let's suppose your foremost ambition is to become wealthy. Wealth itself is relative, of course, so merely expressing your desires in a phrase such as 'I want to be wealthy' really isn't saying much at all. Is that wealthy as compared to someone living on the street, as compared to your current situation, or as compared to someone who is 'financially independent' (another pretty vague description)?

If we turn that vague want into a 'well-formed outcome' then it becomes far more focused, and therefore far more achievable.

I want to be wealthy, and I'll know that I'm wealthy when:

■ I hear people around me talking about my beautiful country home, my smart clothes and my top of the range sports car.

■ I see that my bank balance always exceeds £1 million.

■ I feel relaxed, comfortable and unpressured at all times.

Notice that an outcome is *always* expressed in positive statements. 'I don't want to be poor' or 'I never want to have to work again' may accurately describe your viewpoint, but they leave you facing an *undesirable* state and away from the *desired* state. 'I'll know that I am wealthy when...' implies a positive progression, a sequence of improvements leading to the achievement of the desired state.

In the earlier example, the sales director would almost certainly achieve more lasting results if he set some precise targets:

This time next year I want to be able to announce that our sales for the year went over the £17 million mark. I want to see every one of you better your year-on-year figures by at least 15 per cent.

I feel proud to be at the head of such a professional team. Together we *can* do it. I *believe* we can do it. I *know* we can do it!

To fume, or not to fume

As we saw in Chapter 2, our emotional reactions are actually based on our *perceptions* of the events we encounter. Let's apply that knowledge to a practical situation.

Imagine that you are the production manager of a light engineering company which makes, amongst other things, oven doors for a leading manufacturer of kitchen appliances. How might you react to the following events?

▣ You arrive at the office one morning and the senior supervisor tells you that production in his department will stop before the end of the day shift because they are running out of handles.

▣ The supervisor in the press shop reports reduced output because there were six absentees on the night shift, and they are also running short of the metal 'blanks' which are made into handles.

▣ The stock controller says more sheet metal has been ordered but the supplier reports that several lorry drivers are off sick and they can't deliver in less than two to three days.

So, what would *you* do?

You could get very angry, shout and curse at your own people and then phone up the suppliers and threaten to sue them for breach of contract if they don't deliver the ordered material by the end of the day. If you set this down as an outcome it would presumably look something like this.

I want to:

▣ see everyone rushing around like a load of bluebottles in a jam jar, trying to make something out of nothing;

▣ hear lots of excuses and arguments and later on have the MD asking why customers aren't getting their deliveries in time;

▣ feel totally frustrated and get a sore throat from shouting at everyone.

Taking control

An alternative outcome might go like this.

I want to:

▣ see the production line running to schedule and goods going out of the door on time;

■   hear the supervisors telling me that everything is running smoothly, and the sales department telling me the customer has decided to place more orders because they are so pleased with the quality of the work and the prompt deliveries;

■   feel calm and in control. I am able to respond appropriately and creatively in any crisis.

With this attitude you can begin to identify the key requirement in this situation – to get hold of some raw stock to feed the presses so that the production line can keep going. With a little thought you come up with a suitable solution. For example, you telephone your suppliers and confirm that the sheet metal is ready to be delivered. Then you call up a local haulier and arrange for a lorry to fetch the material as soon as possible.

Being realistic, maybe the raw materials still won't arrive in time to keep the production line running till the end of the day, but it'll be back on stream tomorrow. You may have to pay some overtime if you need someone to unload the lorry outside normal hours. And maybe you'll have to contact a staff agency to get a full quota of operators in the press shop tonight.

Yet even with all these drawbacks you'll still be better off than if you simply stomp around venting your anger on everyone in sight.

Impressive results

There have been a number of goal-setting acronyms circulating in the business world at one time or another – such as **SMART**, which stood for: Specific, Measurable, Achievable, Realistic and Timely. And since NLP addresses the task of setting what are called 'well-formed outcomes', it also defines specific requirements for that process. Strangely enough, however, there is no single acronym for the NLP process. So here's one I prepared earlier:

■ Individual. As far as possible, your goals should be things that you can achieve more or less by your own efforts. The more your goals rely on other people's actions, agreement, co-operation, etc, the more chances there are for you to lose control of the process and end up with results that, at best, only approximate to your intended outcome.

■ Measurable. You need to be able to define, in advance, the criteria you will use to determine when you have achieved your goal. These measures both act as a way of gauging, at any moment, whether your task is complete and also help you to ensure that you are 'progressing' in the right direction.

■ Positive. In order to stay focused on achieving your goal you need to have some kind of representation of the goal inside your head – a mental map, in fact. And, since you cannot make a mental map of a negative, it must be created in the positive in order to be effective.

■ Realistic. Bearing in mind whatever time and resources you have available, what can you realistically hope to achieve? Sometimes this part of goal setting can be very frustrating because you begin to realise that the goal you wanted to aim for isn't realistic. To resolve the problem and avoid that frustration, simply break your overall goal down into smaller chunks (see Chapter 13) – a series of lesser goals, each of which is realistic in its own right, and each of which contributes to the realisation of that greater goal.

■ Ecological. Pause for a moment and imagine that you have already achieved your goal. How does everything around you look, sound and feel? Whilst you have successfully achieved your goal, have you discovered any 'downside' to the situation? Is there anything you can alter about the way you achieved your goal that would improve the situation? Are there any other people or plans you forgot to take into consideration? And even if things are OK in the short term, can you detect any way in which achieving your current goal might interfere with your strategic or long-term goals?

▪ Specific. The more specific you can make your goal the easier it will be to determine what you need to do to attain that goal, and whether you are staying on track to achieve your intended outcome. This in turn makes it far more likely that you will achieve a satisfactory conclusion. For example, most of us have wished we were rich, at one time or another, and maybe we even dreamt about what it would be like – a 'nice' house, a 'brand new' car, holidays at 'exotic' locations, and so on. And how many of us have realised those dreams? Not many.

Film star Jim Carrey, on the other hand, is reputed to have written himself a cheque, when he first started acting, for $10 million. He kept the cheque in his wallet and, whenever things weren't going too well, he took the cheque out, looked at it and put it away again. Until the day came when he signed a contract giving him $10 million for a single film: *The Mask*. On that day he took the cheque out, tore it up and threw it away.

▪ Sustainable. And finally, unless your goal is intended to be short-term, make sure you have a real chance of keeping your plan going in the long term as well. There is no way of telling how many new businesses start up and fail within a matter of a year or two, or even less, because the would-be entrepreneur(s) only considered what was necessary to get a cherished project up and running, with little or no thought as to how they were going to manage it on a day-to-day basis. *The Millennium Dome* in South London (or 'Greenwich Gumboil', as it has been called) is possibly one of the most famous *un*sustainable projects of modern times.

Checking off any new plan or project against a list like this cannot *guarantee* success, of course, but it gives us a far better chance of anticipating potential trouble spots than if we simply launch into a new project, feet first, with not even a hint of a proverbial 'Plan B' waiting in the background.

Checkpoint actions

1. Again, listen to conversations between people at work, but this time aim to detect each person's PTS.
2. Once you think that you have identified someone's PTS, see what happens if you match that PTS – and then deliberately shift into a different PTS.
   (Only do this with someone who won't take offence if they spot what you are doing.)
3. Is there a specific state of mind – calmness, confidence, creativity or whatever – which you would like to be able to access at will?

▨ Think back to a time when you were in that state.

▨ Take note of your feelings (emotional and physical), what you heard and saw and even anything you smelt or tasted.

▨ Make your mental pictures as large, bright and focused as possible, make the sounds clear and audible, let your posture reflect what you are feeling, and so on.
This *must* be done in an 'associated' state. (In NLP all personal experiences are identified as 'associated' (you are involved in the event), or 'dissociated' (you are watching the event as an outside observer).)

▨ As the experience becomes really strong, touch yourself briefly but firmly behind your left ear lobe with your left forefinger.

▨ Repeat the process several times, then test the link by repeating the physical gesture whilst thinking about something quite different.

▨ Repeat the entire cycle until the physical gesture immediately calls up the positive memories. (This may take several attempts when you first try it, but you will find that the results are well worth the effort.)

7

Building relationships

The vital link

It is commonly accepted that the success of *any* person-to-person communication, for any purpose, depends on the extent to which rapport exists between the people involved. And generally speaking, when we talk about rapport we mean things like trust, harmony, etc. In NLP terms, however, these things are the *consequence* of establishing rapport – they are not themselves rapport. From the NLP perspective, rapport is the process of establishing and maintaining contact with a person at a *non*-conscious level.

The value of making contact at a non-conscious level is that it bypasses the various, often very arbitrary, filters we exercise at the conscious level. It must be said, however, that this is something of a two-edged sword (it cuts both ways!).

An example of the positive effects of rapport would be a situation I encountered on an 'outward bound'-style course for trainee managers, some years ago. None of the people on the course had met before, and one team of four seemed to spend the entire course, at the conscious level, arguing with each other, as they jockeyed for position within the group. You might expect that with so much bickering going on they would have ruined their chances as a team in the various competitions that were staged during the course. But not a bit of it. Despite their outward appearance of disagreement, the four young men established an underlying rapport so that they were able to appear to disagree and at the same time work together so effectively as a team that they came first in nearly every activity.

That may be a somewhat extreme case, but this non-conscious inclination to co-operate is actually quite commonplace. Indeed, as Sue Knight explains in her book *NLP at Work:* 'Most business decisions are made on the basis of rapport rather than technical merit.' This fact was neatly illustrated in an article in *Computing* magazine which dealt with the selection of IT training:

> As many as 91% of respondents said suppliers were selected by word of mouth, rather than a structured evaluation based on supplier presentations...

I am not a number...

Rapport isn't only important at the person-to-person level. As many major corporations have discovered, when a company exceeds a certain size, or is distributed over a number of separate sites, effective centralised management becomes nigh on impossible and internal cohesiveness begins to suffer.

Without rapport, management style tends to become either inflexible and bureaucratic, or fragmented and vague. In either case the company will reflect the negative effects in its overall performance, yet it seems that there are still plenty of companies which clearly do not understand the significance of rapport. Indeed, in the early to mid-1990s we saw the arrival of a whole new set of jargon which, though intended to denote greater efficiency, really only served to create greater divisiveness in the workplace.

It is a basic tenet of NLP that the language we use will both reflect and shape the way we think about the world around us.

Take a look at the short list of terms below and see which column *you* think is more likely to promote rapport:

A	B
HR (Human Resources)	People
HRD (Human Resource Development)	Training/Education
O&R (Organisation and Resources)	Personnel Department

I am a free man!

NLP is about *increasing* people's effectiveness and *maximising* their potential. Moreover, in contrast with many recent developments in the business world, NLP achieves its results by fostering individuality, in a constructive manner.

BPR (business process re-engineering), with its emphasis on tighter controls, downsizing, cost-cutting exercises, and so on, has done much to devalue the role of the individual within the organisation. Yet despite all the hyperbole, BPR failed to deliver the goods. Even supporters of BPR concede that less than 1 per cent of corporations were fully re-engineered, and that the failure rate for BPR projects may have been as high as 95 per cent!

Why? Because BPR is about theories, not people. According to James Champy, co-author of *Re-engineering the Corporation*:

> ... within the past five years we have trained a generation of managers who believe that a company is developed by reducing costs. If re-engineering only takes a cost focus, there's a high risk that it will reduce the capability and capacity of the organization. People can't survive in companies that are shrinking.

As the degree of rapport in the work environment goes down, so the work itself quickly seems to lose its intrinsic value and employees become increasingly alienated. As one professional told me, as though it was patently obvious: 'Work is what you do to make the money to do what you really want to do.'

Turning the tide

Rapport is the antidote to all of these negative factors. At an individual level it allows us to create more effective personal relationships, easily and quickly, even with complete strangers.

At a company level rapport provides a basis for effective empowerment and optimal working relationships between staff and management, between departments, and so on.

Rapport can also improve customer relations – if you take the trouble to show people that you respect their beliefs and values. This does not mean that you have to share those values and beliefs, only that you acknowledge them in a positive manner.

Karen Boylston, a director of the Centre for Creative Leadership, confirms the fact that this is a key business issue:

> Customers are telling businesses, 'I don't care if every member of your staff graduated with honours from Harvard, Stanford and Wharton [top US business colleges]. I will take my business and go where I am understood and treated with respect.'

Another aspect of rapport, then, is the ability to show someone that you 'understand and respect them as a human being'.

The time and the place

It is worth saying that the best relationships come about when we use rapport to create interaction at an *appropriate* level.

In a family context it would be appropriate to develop a very deep or very warm relationship. In a romantic relationship the level of rapport might run to passionate or even red-hot. In a business context, however, it is quite sufficient to develop a relationship of mutual respect.

It is also important to recognise that we may need to vary the level of rapport we use with a particular person or group, depending on the context. If we utilise rapport beyond a certain level we run the danger of leading the other party to imagine that there is more to the relationship than we want or intend.

The 'word of mouth' selection process referred to earlier has, at its heart, a favourable assessment of the trainers/training. But is it really appropriate to award contracts or select suppliers purely on the basis of how someone else *feels* about it, rather than on the basis of an objective assessment of our business needs? Conducting business on the basis of our rapport with a third party is arguably just as likely to create problems as if we had no rapport at all.

Taking this one step further, in a negotiating situation, for example, it may be beneficial to gently *break* rapport before you make an important decision. This gives you the opportunity to judge the current position on its business merits rather than simply reaching agreement because you don't want to disturb the warmth that has built up between the parties to the negotiation.

A two-way street?

As I said earlier, connecting with someone at a non-conscious level *can be* a two-edged sword for the other person. And here's the reason why.

The phenomenon known as 'buyer's remorse' shows what happens when we make a decision that is overly influenced by rapport. Some salespeople understand this very well, and aim to deepen the rapport they have with the customer as they go for the 'close'. This is distinctly one-way rapport – the salesperson is communicating with the customer's unconscious, which is fine, if it really is in the customer's interest to complete the sale. But if the ploy is simply being used to make the sale, however, there is real danger that the customer will regret the purchase – and may come to believe that the salesperson has betrayed them – which is hardly a healthy basis for any future dealings!

This is also very relevant in training situations, an important investment area for many companies.

It seems to be widely believed, both by training companies and by their clients, that a trainer who scores well on post-course evaluation sheets must therefore be a good trainer. Studies have shown, however, that trainers who consistently score better than an 80 per cent approval rating are possibly being scored on their ability to create rapport with the trainees – their *social* skills – rather than on the effectiveness of the training they provide.

A trainer whose evaluations score 61–80 per cent may be establishing a less intense, but more appropriate, degree of rapport and consequently providing more effective training as measured by results three, six or nine months after the course is over.

Checkpoint action

In the next two chapters we will be looking at some specific techniques for developing rapport.

For the moment you might like to simply watch how people around you relate to each other and see if you can spot any behaviour patterns which are common to:

    a.   situations with a medium to high level of rapport;
    b.   situations where rapport is low or even non-existent.

8

Talking body language

Matching and mirroring

Amongst the NLP techniques that can be used to create rapport are *matching* and *mirroring* the other person's behaviour.

The technique is called 'matching and mirroring' because you set yourself up as a 'mirror' for the other person by matching that person's behaviour, directly or indirectly, to varying degrees.

When dealing with groups you will need to match and mirror the person you are currently speaking to, whilst also paying attention to the person you most wish to influence.

The four mirroring techniques are:

- mirroring *voice tone/tempo*;
- mirroring *breathing rate*;
- mirroring *movement*;
- mirroring *body posture*.

These stratagems are particularly effective:

- either as a means of creating rapport when some degree of trust has already been established, or
- deepening an existing level of rapport.

Tone and tempo

In a business context, mirroring voice tone and/or speech tempo is probably the most effective way to establish rapport.

It is relatively difficult to spot since few of us have a very accurate idea of what our own voice sounds like to other people. We are even less aware of how our voices change in various situations – it depends on what we think of the person we are talking to, our current emotional state, and so on.

The *tone* of voice can be high or low, loud or soft, clear or mumbled, etc, while the *tempo* can be fast or slow, flowing or hesitant, variable or monotonous. You need only mirror the *general* characteristics of a person's voice. You need not, and should not, try to do an 'impression' of their voice such as copying an accent, quirky mispronunciations, etc.

Generally speaking, a person in kinaesthetic mode will tend to speak quite slowly, often with very noticeable pauses and in a deeper than average tone. Someone in auditory mode is more likely to have an even-paced, well-modulated, interesting voice, while being in visual mode is often characterised by rapid, rather high-pitched speech.

A breath of familiarity

Mirroring a person's *breathing rate* is a very effective way of establishing rapport, but it is also the most difficult, especially if the other person is wearing baggy clothing, keeps shifting around or, worse yet, appears to have stopped breathing.

As a rough guide, someone in kinaesthetic mode will usually breathe quite regularly and fully, from the bottom of their lungs. A person in auditory mode will also breathe quite regularly, but from the mid-chest area. Whilst in visual mode, people tend to breathe quite lightly using only the upper chest.

If you can't see any chest movement at all, watch for the rise and fall of their shoulders, or use a slow, shallow breathing pattern yourself and watch for a response.

Something in the way you move

Matching *body movement* and *body posture* are the easiest forms of mirroring, but should be used with great discretion.

In its most literal form, I might mirror your posture, movements and gestures quite directly. If *you* lean back, then *I* will lean back; if *you* cross your legs to the left, I will cross *my* legs to the left, and so on. The only difference is that I will leave a pause before copying you, and my movements will be quite slow and subtle. The danger here is that you will detect what I am doing, at least subconsciously, and end up feeling irritation rather than rapport.

One way to avoid this error is to simulate just some aspects of the other person's posture and gestures, leaving a varying amount of time before responding to a given movement.

Alternatively, you could use the 'crossover mirroring' technique. Rather than directly copying the other person's actions you make reciprocal gestures. So, if you are tapping the desk with your pencil, I might drum on my knee with my fingers *at the same tempo*. If you cross your legs I cross my arms, etc.

Once again, the emphasis is on using smooth, discreet, apparently independent movements to avoid giving away the fact that you are actually reacting to the other person.

Watch my hands

Body language is also important in that people often make small but easily discernible movements that effectively 'point out' their preferred thinking style at a particular moment:

■ Rubbing or pointing to the area around the eyes suggests a *visual* mode of thinking. This person may not '*see* what you're getting at'. Or perhaps she has '*spotted* something interesting' in what you just said.

Enhance your communication by using *visual* phrases: 'Let me show you what I mean', 'Let me clarify that idea', 'Let's put that under the microscope', and so on.

▦ Any noticeable movement around the ears or the mouth indicates that *auditory* processing is at work. If someone starts pulling at their earlobe, for example, this may indicate that they don't 'like what they *hear*', or they may be thinking 'there's a lot in what you say'.

You might respond with phrases like: 'Let me tell you what I mean' or 'Let's send a clear message.'

▦ Gestures with the arms and/or hands usually accompany a *kinaesthetic* response. That person may '*feel* that some point needs *fleshing out*', or he may think that your ideas have given him 'something to get to *grips* with'. In which case use lines such as: 'Let's kick this idea around' or 'We need to tackle this without delay.'

In each case it is important to note what responses you are getting. These signals are *indicators*, not rules, so it is important to watch for responsive signals such as smiles, head nods and so on.

Checkpoint actions

See the end of Chapter 9.

9

Follow the leader

Walk this way

As long as you are interacting with another person, whether individually or in a group, you will be either *pacing* or *leading* that other person. That is to say, regardless of how much or how little you know about NLP, you will either:

- behave in a way that is similar to the other person's behaviour (in NLP this is called *pacing*), or
- behave in a way that is quite unlike the other person's behaviour (known as *leading*).

Successful *pacing* goes beyond the matching and mirroring techniques described in Chapter 8. To pace someone really effectively you may also need to detect and mirror their beliefs, values and the content of what they say. (However, you don't have to share those beliefs and values in order to mirror them.) Once your pacing creates a sufficient degree of rapport, you can then move on to start leading the person or people you have been pacing. Thus, you can begin to guide the person you are dealing with rather than being led by them. Indeed, we can use leading to determine the effectiveness of our pacing.

When pacing – creating rapport – is effective we are communicating with the other person/people in the interaction at a level below their conscious attention. At this level they will normally be more responsive, as long as we do not try to act against them in any way. We can test whether we have actually created that responsive state by *initiating* action instead of following the other person's lead. For example, if we are both sitting with our legs crossed, then instead of waiting for you to make a move I will uncross my legs and straighten up in my seat. If I have indeed created rapport then shortly after I make these moves you will make similar moves. If you don't respond that simply means that we aren't yet in strong rapport, and I need to carry on pacing you for a little longer before I make another 'leading move'.

A graphic illustration of this switch from pacing to leading occurred when two colleagues and myself were walking back to our car in the parking lot of a motorway service station. We'd gone about 40 or 50 yards, when the person in the middle suddenly pointed away to the right and asked: 'Why are we walking this way – the car's over there!'

During the relaxed conversation in the restaurant we were effectively pacing each other. When we left the restaurant one person headed for where he *thought* our car was located, and because of the high level of rapport between us, the other two allowed ourselves to be guided *away* from the car, even though it was in full view throughout the incident.

Leading to win

In a business situation, once a significant degree of rapport has been established by matching the other person's behaviour, the pacer should be able to transfer smoothly into leading mode in order to bring the event to its desired conclusion.

But beware. Pacing and leading are only truly effective when both leader *and* those being led are headed towards a win/win situation. A 'leader' who works towards a win/lose conclusion (ie where he wins and they lose) is quite likely to find that the whole manoeuvre falls apart as the 'victims' wake up to the true nature, and consequences, of the transaction.

Are you shouting at me?

This technique can often involve the use of seemingly quite bizarre behaviour. Imagine, for example, that you are dealing with a complaining customer, face to face or over the phone. The customer is already angry, and after a sentence or two she starts shouting at you. What do you do?

Would you keep calm, talk to her in a respectful, hushed tone and generally try to quieten her down? Bad choice!

You have just completely mismatched the customer's voice and body language. Far from validating her hurt feelings, you are implying that there is nothing to get upset about. If there was the least hint of rapport between you to start with, you've almost certainly killed it stone dead.

What, then, should you do? You should *pace* then *lead*. Match the tone, but not the content of what she is saying, then slowly lead her down to a state in which you can work together to resolve the grievance. For example:

Customer (loudly):
Do you see the state this dress is in? I've only worn it twice and it's coming apart. What are you going to do about it? I demand my money back. I wouldn't shop here again if you were the last store in town!

You (matching the tone and part of the body language):
(*Pacing*) I certainly do see what you mean about the dress, and I'm not surprised that you're upset. *I'm* upset! We have a policy in the store of only selling the very best quality clothes. And that garment clearly doesn't meet our standards!

(Slowly calming down – *leading*) You certainly do have grounds for complaint. And that's not the way we want one of our customers to feel when they come to our store. (Calmer still) So I want to do whatever I can to put this right. Because I want you to look on this store as somewhere you can depend on for high quality products.

At this point you should be able to help the customer to reach a mutually acceptable solution.

If the process doesn't work first time – and it may not, if the other person is sufficiently upset – simply pace and lead, pace and lead until they do start to calm down.

Checkpoint actions

1. Spend a few days taking conscious note of the speaking patterns of people you talk to – tone, tempo, etc.
2. Spend a few more days noticing people's body language.
3. In situations where it will not cause offence if anyone realises what you are doing, match and mirror people's vocal characteristics and body language (but don't do a direct imitation of the other person).
4. Notice what difference it makes for you when you adopt someone else's style of speaking and/or physical posture.
5. Watch how pacing and leading occur between people in workplace interactions. Is it always the more senior person who does the leading?
6. Use body movements and voice to create rapport, then see what changes you need to make in order to:
   a. lead the other person;
   b. break rapport.

10

Give the dog a new name

Anchors aweigh!

If you completed all of the Checkpoint Actions for Chapter 6, you will remember how you were able to recall a positive frame of mind by using a simple physical gesture. In NLP this process of creating a mental link between an internal state and an external event is known as anchoring. As you have already discovered, an anchor is a *learned* response, which means that we can create, alter and dissolve anchors, at will, in order to achieve specific results.

The higher the fewer

Unfortunately, we can also, quite unintentionally, create inappropriate anchors. For example, in many companies today, the higher you go up the management ladder, the fewer people you will find who have any great length of service in that company, except those at the very top, perhaps.

It is as though the companies have developed such a negative view of the link between loyalty and competence that the only way to get promoted is to leave.

Why do companies act this way? At first sight such behaviour may seem somewhat self-defeating, yet it does prove to make sense if we relate it to the NLP concept of anchoring.

Just as a particular feeling can be anchored to a particular piece of music, so our feelings about a particular person can become anchored to a specific situation, such as seeing that person in the same role day after day, month after month.

When this kind of unconscious, unintentional anchoring occurs, when we label someone by their job title (or their sex, or their skin colour), instead of seeing them as a unique individual, or when we evaluate them according to past performance, instead of according to what they are doing now, they can become anchored (in our thoughts) to a particular response. Once this happens it can take something like a resignation before we can clear the anchors and recognise that person's true worth.

Companies with a clear pattern of 'promotion through resignation' need to look very closely at the company culture. Some training in basic people skills may be long overdue.

The same problem exists when we characterise a person by judgemental labels ('maverick', 'loner', etc), as though the person and their behaviour are the same thing. That is to say, when we 'give a dog a bad name'.

Put very simply, we tend to see what we *expect* to see, so when we give someone a label we severely limit our own ability to take an objective view of that person. Moreover, whilst people cannot change what they 'are', we can change our *behaviour* in any way we want, whenever we want. The biggest barrier to change is usually not in the individual, but in other people's refusal to accept that change might be possible.

A rose by any other name

We also need to pause here to consider just *how* the way in which we use words – and especially 'labels' – can heavily influence the way we think about things.

Take the term 'maverick', for example. For one person this may have negative connotations – someone who is difficult to handle, who is always off doing what he wants instead of fitting in like a good 'team player'. But is this the meaning that the 'maverick' will pick up on? Remember that the title of the autobiography of South America's most famous, and successful, industrialist, Ricardo Semler, is *Maverick!*

Indeed, many business books readily acknowledge that a few 'mavericks' are essential to the well-being of any company precisely because they do routinely challenge the status quo.

So what may be intended as a term of disapproval to the person saying it may sound like a commendation to the person it is directed to. Result? Instead of discouraging unwanted behaviour, using labels in place of constructive discussion may actually re-inforce the very behaviour it was meant to deter.

Inadvertent hypnosis

There is now substantial evidence that we all tend to drift in and out of a 'trance state' on a regular basis throughout our waking hours. During these incidents, which occur every 90 minutes and last for some 15–20 minutes (both timings are approximate), we may find that we are clumsier, more easily distracted and more suggestible. This pattern of trances, known as the *ultradian rhythm*, seems to be our intuitive way of taking time to process incoming information.

The existence of these trances illustrates our ability to enter 'altered states of consciousness' in a very easy and natural manner, and helps to explain what I call 'inadvertent hypnosis'.

Suppose, for a moment, that you have the job of helping someone learn to ride a bike. Would you tell them:

■ 'Keep it steady'; or
■ 'Don't let it wobble.'

The difference between these two phrases may seem trivial in the extreme, yet in the real world the first instruction will be heard as a positive and supportive command, whilst the second is an invitation to disaster. The point to note here is that the human brain often cannot hear *exactly* what is being said.

Don't think about a blue elephant

OK, are you *not* thinking about a blue elephant? Of course you aren't. It just isn't possible to know whether you are *not* thinking about something unless you think about that thing in order to know what it is you're not going to think about!

Since the human brain simply cannot think in negatives, if I say 'Don't let it wobble' the listener must first think about wobbling in order to know what it is they shouldn't do – and will probably wobble all over the place in the process. But if I say 'Keep it steady', no such complications arise and the trainee can choose to do precisely that.

Checkpoint actions

1. As you meet with friends and colleagues, be aware of the extent to which your reactions are based on past events. Are you really seeing people as they are *now*, or as they used to be?
2. When decisions have to be made, to what extent do you choose to do things 'the way we've always done them'? Are you losing out on efficiency and creativity by refusing to accept the need for, and likely benefits of, change?

11

When you put it like that

It's the way you tell 'em

Two people say almost exactly the same thing, yet one version sounds like a threat, and one is a simple comment.

Why? Because everything that happens, happens 'in context'. When someone speaks to us we take account of who they are, what we think about them, and so on. If a friend telephones and says 'Have you got a minute?' in a cheery tone of voice, that will have totally different connotations compared with a situation where your boss ambushes you as you pass his office and asks in a sombre tone 'Have you got a minute?'

The meaning of what you say is the response that it gets.

In NLP jargon, everything we say and do occurs within what is referred to as a 'frame'. We've all been in a situation when, for no apparent reason, people responded to us in a way that was totally at odds with our intentions. It's as though they were responding to the frame instead of to the picture.

For example, you might be in a meeting where some future

event is being planned and you make what you think is quite obviously a suggestion. One of the other people in the meeting turns on you, however, and criticises you for being so pushy and for not waiting to see what everyone else has to say.

Quite possibly what has happened here is that you have been talking about the event using the 'as if' frame ('as if' the event had actually happened as you described) without making it clear that it was meant to be purely speculative.

What will they hear when you speak?

So, an effective frame is more than just another way of saying something – it must also get your listener(s) to 'see' whatever it is you're talking about in a new way. For example:

> It isn't easy for me to say this, because I know it may sound unpleasant, and it may seem as though I haven't given you credit for all the hard work that you've put into preparing this presentation. It is my job to make sure that we show ourselves to our customers in the best possible light. And because of that I'm going to ask you to go back and rework this presentation.
>
> It needs to be shorter and punchier – not more than 40–45 minutes, maximum – and I want you to replace the jargon with language that the customer will understand.
>
> Is that clear?

This explanation gives what might otherwise seem like naked criticism and frames it in terms of 'what we need to show the customer'. This shows that you've given some thought to how your comments might be perceived.

Notice the use of the word 'because' towards the end of the first paragraph. Although no one seems to know why, an explanation, even a weak one, often appears far more persuasive if it includes the word 'because'.

The second paragraph – 'It needs...' – offers some constructive guidelines for improvement, and also shows that you've given the matter some thought rather than just reacting.

Lastly, 'Is that clear?' is ambiguous enough to be answered yes or no, or to open the way for more discussion, if necessary. Requests can also benefit by being well framed, with the *reason* for the request coming *before* the request itself:

> I don't know if you're aware of this fact – a recent internal study showed that it takes a programmer several days to produce a single page for the company website. And even then the result often leaves a lot to be desired.
>
> There's a graphic design package I've been looking at which allows the user to create pages as good as or better than the ones we have in a fraction of the time and in such a way that we could change things like the font, background colour and so on with just a couple of clicks of a mouse button. It can even check the spelling and grammar – and we know from experience how important that can be. It's pretty expensive, but I believe it could pay for itself in a few weeks.
>
> That's why I'm suggesting that we provide each member of the website team with a copy of this program.

Apart from a hint of a request at the start of the third paragraph, it is only after some very relevant advantages have been described that we finally find out what the speaker is actually asking for. The listener cannot reasonably respond to the request until it has been clearly specified – in the final sentence!

But suppose the speaker had started out in reverse order:

> I'm putting in this request to supply the website designers with copies of a graphics design program.
>
> I don't know if you're aware of this fact – a recent internal study showed that it takes a programmer several days...

This way round, the listener can make a decision immediately and totally ignore the explanation, no matter how good.

Sweetening the pill

About 70–80 per cent of the population tend to be resistant to change, to a greater or lesser extent. This means that the way in which news of a change is presented is often crucial to successful implementation of that change. Here again, framing can make the difference between success and failure.

When introducing new technology, for example, salesmen and enthusiasts tend to use phrases like:

■ 'It's a whole *new way* of working.'
■ 'This will *revolutionise* working practices.'
■ 'These are the machines *of the future*.'

Imagine how these phrases must sound to someone who is averse to change. No wonder so many people, including many managers, still show signs of technophobia.

How much easier would it be if the new technology was introduced within a more sensitive frame, such as:

■ 'A way to make your job *easier*.'
■ 'In most respects, *as straightforward as* using a typewriter.'
■ '*Full training* will be provided.'

By changing the phrasing, the changes become *evolutionary* rather than *revolutionary*, and much less threatening.

On the other hand...

Where framing *creates* a context, reframing *reshapes* the context. It is a way of reviewing an existing situation or idea so that the content can be re-evaluated. It can be a very powerful way of expanding someone's understanding of their existing map of a particular situation.

Long-termism versus short-termism in business is just one example of how reframing has become a badly needed skill.

In the world of computer programming, for instance, there has been a trend towards:

■ shedding permanent staff;
■ making increasing use of contract labour.

In the short term this has at least two important advantages:

▓ Contractors only need be employed as long as there is work for them to do.
▓ Specialist skills can be bought in when needed rather than paying for regular staff to be trained up.

If we reframe the action, however, we see that there are limitations as well as advantages:

▓ Contractors don't have the same loyalty or self-interest in the success of the company as do permanent staff members.
▓ If your systems have been developed by a group of people who have all moved on, who is there in-house who really understands what it's all about?

The initial frame seemed very attractive, and was correct, as far as it went. Only by reframing the possible outcomes can we appreciate both the advantages and the drawbacks of each alternative, decide whether the action is still worth taking, and, if it is, how we can minimise any negative side effects.

Trouble is a state of mind

This can be particularly effective when we apply reframing in order to review what appear to be 'problem' situations.

An important reframe that many companies have yet to understand concerns customer relationships. Customer-facing staff complain that customers want everything, yesterday, and preferably for free. And it's true; some customers can be difficult. And then again, without any customers, where's your business?

The reframe on this point is simply this: 'If all customers can be difficult at one time or another, then having difficulties with customers is an integral part of running a successful business. Difficult customers aren't really a burden at all – they are proof of success!'

Checkpoint actions

1. You have to ask someone to re-do a task when there really isn't any excuse for not having done it properly the first time round.
    - How would you frame your comments to get a positive response?
    - How do you feel about trying to be positive when the other person is so clearly at fault?

    Repeat this exercise with several different work colleagues in mind.
    Is there a difference depending on the person you have in mind? If so, why?

2. Make it a habit, whenever you hear a negative comment, to look for a striking reframe. For example:

    Comment: 'I hate getting up at 7.00 am every morning!'
    Reframe: 'You wouldn't have that problem if you didn't have a job – and the salary that goes with it.'

    Do this in response to your own negative thoughts.

12

Meta programs and motivation

'Quick fix' thinking

Years ago, one of the managers I was working with at the time came back from an interpersonal skills workshop and announced that he had made a major discovery: 'You can't motivate other people, and it's a waste of time trying.'

Well, if motivating someone means getting them so fired up that they'll work flat out for the next 50 years with no further intervention then no, you cannot motivate another person.

If, on the other hand, we're talking about understanding what gets another person excited, or turned off, so that we can encourage them to follow or avoid a certain course of action, then we certainly can motivate other people quite effectively.

We all have certain set ways of thinking – predefined or 'preprogrammed' ways of viewing and reacting to the events going on around us – which we often use as a way of streamlining our interactions with our surroundings rather than going through the comparatively lengthy business of rational thinking. The downside of such 'quick fix' thinking is that sometimes the programs take over. And that's when, for example, gooey love stories and lurid melodramas can bring us close to tears even when, intellectually, we know that what we are looking at is pure fiction.

In NLP these filters are known as *meta programs*, and when we know which *meta programs* a person works to in a given situation we can frame our communication accordingly.

Meta programs, like other ideas in NLP, work best when we deal with people as they *are* – not as we think they *should* be.

Perceptions, thoughts and emotions

In order to appreciate the role of meta programs it is essential that we understand the relationship between perceptions, thoughts and emotions. For example, if our perceptions shape our emotions, what shapes our perceptions? The latest evidence suggests that they are filtered and re-evaluated according to our previous experiences, beliefs, values and knowledge.

If we recognise which filters people are using, we can anticipate how they are likely to react to what we do and say.

NLP time

The first two meta programs are to do with how people experience time, and are unlike most other meta programs in that people tend to be fairly consistent as regards their attitude towards time. It should also be noted that both of these meta programs tend to work at a cultural as well as an individual level.

Inside time–outside time

This meta program describes how people arrange their perception of events past, present and future. The two options are often referred to as *through time* and *in time*, but the labels are used here more accurate and easier to remember.

Inside time describes someone who becomes caught up in the stream of events in their lives. They can only 'see' events in the immediate future and the immediate past, which tend to be straight in front of them and right behind them, respectively. This makes it difficult for someone *inside time* to look objectively over past events, plan ahead, estimate the time required to complete a task or turn up on time.

Someone in *outside time* mode, however, 'sees' events as something like a stream flowing past in front of them. They are better able to view the past and plan ahead and thus see how events are developing.

People who operate *inside time* are often excellent workers, able to sustain their concentration for long periods of time. Unfortunately this is liable to get them promoted to a managerial position – for which they are totally unsuited as such roles require the abilities that go with an *outside time* perspective.

Monochronic–polychronic

An essential aspect of assigning roles in any company is knowing which people are task-oriented and which are people-oriented. According to sociologist Edward Hall, a person in *monochronic* mode takes time very seriously, likes to do one thing at a time – without interruptions – is a stickler for promptness, and tends to be rather inflexible once a plan is in place.

Someone in *polychronic* mode, on the other hand, will usually prefer to multi-task, love interruptions and diversions, and see appointment times as rough guidelines.

People who prefer *monochronic* mode are well suited to task-oriented roles, while people who prefer *polychronic* mode are 'people people', best suited to roles in PR, corporate hospitality and the like.

Towards–away from

When someone says: 'I'm going to do xyz *because...*', listen very carefully to what comes next – it will tell you whether (in that particular context) their motivation is to work *towards* or *away from* the stated result.

A person in *towards* mode thinks in positive terms, identifying what they want to achieve. They have an image in their mind of what they want and they move more or less directly towards the realisation of their goals. If the *towards* attitude is too strong it can seem aggressive and insensitive rather than assertive.

A person in *away from* mode, on the other hand, thinks in negative terms, with their attention firmly fixed on what they *don't* want. They are much clearer about what they are trying to avoid than about what they want to achieve, and this inability to express a positive desire can make it very hard for them to formulate any kind of outcome (Chapter 6).

For motivation purposes a person in *towards* mode needs to be pointed in the right direction and given their head (with occasional discreet checking to ensure that they stay on course).

A person in *away from* mode can be motivated by threats, but take care, if the threats become too intense they may become afraid to do anything at all.

Options–procedures

As the names suggest, someone in *options* mode thrives in a setting where they have freedom of choice, while a person in *procedures* mode is more inclined to stick to tried and tested lines of action.

When they are in *options* mode, many people have a strong streak of creativity, which they may find difficult to control. They dislike following standard procedures, preferring to find their own way from A to B, quite possibly with diversions to C, D, E and F.

When someone is in *procedures* mode they will probably be happiest when surrounded by standards and a clearly defined course of action. In contrast to the person in *options* mode, they find choices distracting, and given half a chance they will follow a set policy to the bitter end, often with no regard for the consequences. The 'Jobsworth' ('I can't do that, it's more than my job's worth!') is an extreme version of a person who has adopted *procedures* mode behaviour. Bob, in the example in Chapter 3, was certainly in 'procedures mode' in that particular context.

A person in *options* mode really doesn't need motivating as self-motivation is one of their main strengths; rather they need to be kept firmly (but not too obviously) on track.

A person in *procedures* mode is best motivated if they are given detailed instructions, the need to make choices is minimised, and they can earn praise when they adhere to the standard procedures.

Proactive–reactive

People who operate in *proactive* mode are the ultimate self-motivators, the people who are regularly one step ahead of their colleagues. On the downside they will often ignore the analysis and planning which are needed when making important decisions.

By way of contrast, people who feel more comfortable in *reactive* mode are often noted for their love of collecting information and careful planning before doing anything at all. In *proactive* mode, collecting information is done as part of an overall planning process; in *reactive* mode it is more likely to be used as a delaying tactic because they would really rather do nothing at all. That is to say, to avoid commitment and responsibility, *not* because they are lazy.

In *proactive* mode, people need very little motivation, though they can be turned off if they perceive that their initiatives are being rejected or unduly criticised. *Reactive* mode is better suited to group situations, where people have very little individual responsibility, and when they have a clear idea of what they are required to do and why.

By the way, *proactive* mode really isn't the best choice in every situation. Although the business world is awash with 'entrepreneur' – types demanding that everyone be *proactive*, a whole team of people in *proactive* mode is no team at all – just a collection of individuals 'doing their own thing' with minimum consultation, if any.

Convincer evidence

If I want to sell you a product or a certain course of action, how should I present my information to you to make it convincing?

These are four known ways of collecting or presenting evidence to make it convincing, with the first and second 'channels' being the most frequently used:

▪ **Visually:** The person must be able to literally *see* the information in order to be convinced (true for about 55 per cent of the population in a business context).

▪ **Aurally:** The person must be able to *hear* the evidence, in a presentation, by word-of-mouth recommendation or whatever (applies to about 30 per cent of business people).

▪ **Activity:** The evidence must be presented in a way that allows 'hands on' experience of the product or service (true for about 12 per cent of the business community).

▪ **Reading:** The evidence must be delivered in written or printed format so that the person can read it for themself (true for about 3 per cent of the business population).

This part of the decision-making process obviously relates to the main PTSs that were discussed in Chapters 5 and 17. A second aspect of the process deals with how often the evidence must be presented to make it convincing.

Convincer frequency

If you were thinking of investing money in a business, how many times would you need to see details of that business to be convinced that it was a good investment? As with convincer evidence, four main groups have been identified:

▨ **Automatic:** These people make their minds up in no time flat, often on very little information.
▨ **Several times:** People in this group need to see the evidence several times, though the precise number (usually less than 10) will depend on the person and the situation.
▨ **Consistent:** These people are never fully convinced and need regular confirmation that their decision was correct.
▨ **Period of time:** People in this group need to have things repeated over a given period of time rather than on a specific number of occasions. Here, too, the precise length of time will vary according to the person and the situation.

Sameness–difference

Look at the pattern below and, as quickly as you can, write down a brief description of how the shapes are related.

Someone in *sameness* mode would see that all three shapes are the same, possibly with the qualification that the triangle in the centre is upside down. To people in *sameness* mode the similarities they see in the world around them are more important than the differences, though they may acknowledge the differences as an afterthought.

People in *difference* mode, however, will note the differences before anything else, even if they then go on to notice similarities. These people might describe the figure thus: 'Two shapes are pointing upwards, and the middle shape is pointing downwards – Oh, and all three shapes are triangles.'

People in 'sameness–difference' mode can be described using five basic headings:

1. sameness;
2. sameness with qualification;
3. no clear preference;
4. difference with qualification;
5. difference.

As far as motivation is concerned, someone in *sameness* mode naturally responds to conformity, traditional standards and ways of doing things, rather than to newness and innovation.

People in *difference* mode, and the two 'with qualification' groups, are more likely to appreciate 'newness', 'freshness', 'progress' and 'improvement' (try watching TV adverts with this thought in mind!). The closer you get to the unqualified *difference* group, the greater the attraction of newness and innovation for their own sake.

Internal–external

Also known as the 'frame of reference' filter, the *internal–external* meta program is concerned with how people make judgements about their own actions. If you ask someone: 'How do you know when you've done well at a given task?', they may answer that they go by other people's reactions (eg peer pressure), that they have some kind of internal yardstick or that they use some combination of the two:

1. external reference;
2. external reference with internal check;
3. balanced;
4. internal reference with external check;
5. internal reference.

People with a significant element of *external* reference are relatively easy to motivate since your approval, or disapproval, will directly affect their perception of whether they are performing well. Indeed, they can sometimes seem over-responsive, because someone in *external* mode will often hear other people's input, even mild suggestions or queries, as commands.

People with an *internal* frame of reference are really only interested in their own opinions. Where someone in *external* mode hears input as commands, a person in *internal* mode hears external input, even direct commands, as mere information. These people may be hard to motivate unless you frame your approach in the appropriate terms (see the section later in this chapter on *modal operators*).

Gentle persuasion

It is especially important, when discussing motivation, to bear in mind the fact that manipulation invariably fails, sooner or later.

The basic guidelines described in this chapter will only be truly effective when they are used to the benefit of the person *being* motivated, as well as for the person or organisation *doing* the motivating.

Modal operators

These motivating/demotivating phrases are often very powerful simply because they are habitual. A person can learn a modal operator in their childhood and go on using it for life, never questioning whether it has outlasted its usefulness.

The most frequently encountered operators include:

▥ can–can't;
▥ could–couldn't;
▥ must–must not (mustn't);
▥ necessary–unnecessary;
▥ need to–don't need to;
▥ ought–ought not;
▥ possible–impossible;
▥ should–shouldn't;
▥ will–won't.

Although the modal operators are not, strictly speaking, meta programs, they do work in a similar manner. You can only use these operators for motivating someone if you know which pairs of operators have significance for them, of course, but you can often find this with just a little careful listening. For example, if you suggest a certain course of action and the reply comes back: 'I *wouldn't* think so – it *looks impossible*', you won't get far with: 'But we must!' or 'Well, I really think you should.' A far more effective response would be: 'OK, I can *see* why you might think it was *impossible* for some people, but for you I think it *looks* like it *would* be *possible*.'

Corporate meta programs

Meta programs can also be found as the foundations of company culture. A company which finds it difficult to be innovative may be locked into *procedures* mode, whilst a company that is high on creativity, but is never more than a step away from bankruptcy, may be too heavily *options* oriented. Likewise, a company with a genuine emphasis on personal development usually has a *towards* culture, whilst an *away from* company is often characterised by the undue amount of 'fire-fighting' that goes on.

Checkpoint actions

1. Check your own meta programs. Starting with the list given in this chapter, make a quick note of what you guess is your own position on each program – then take a few days to find out what you actually do, in the work context.
2. What do the results of this exercise tell you? Remember that once you know what you actually do, you have the freedom to change anything you think could be improved on.
3. Notice what meta program positions are encouraged in your company. Are there any incongruences – like claiming that innovation is highly valued whilst marginalising anyone who tries to show some initiative? If so, can these incongruences be brought out into the open and dealt with?

13

Making information make sense

Bottom lines and aerial views

You may want to answer the following questions before you read on. It will make the practical application of the information in this chapter much easier to understand.

Q1. When learning about something new, do you prefer to (**A**) start with an overview and work down to specific details, or (**B**) build up to the overall view, detail by detail?

If you chose option **A** then answer **Q2**, otherwise answer **Q3**.

Q2. Are you (**C**) really interested in detailed information, or would you (**D**) prefer to stick with the overview?
Q3. Are you (**E**) really interested in the 'big picture', or would you (**F**) prefer to stick with the details?

Q1	Q2	Q3	Chunk type
A	D	–	Abstract
A	C	–	Abstract to Specific
B	–	F	Specific
B	–	E	Specific to Abstract

Up the down staircase

An important element in Alfred Korzybski's *General Semantics* was what he called the 'ladder of abstraction'. One of the main reasons why we fail to communicate effectively, Korzybski said, was because we so often use *vague* language, and expect other people to understand *precisely* what we mean.

Sometimes this isn't particularly important. If I say that I'm going to London next week, by train, it really doesn't matter whether you understand that I plan to travel first class on the 8.43am Intercity Express from King's Sittingbourne next Friday and will return the same day, or you just think 'London, by train'. But suppose that I want to buy a ticket for that journey – and you are the ticket clerk. In that case it matters a great deal whether you understand exactly what I've planned, because the precise combination of these details will determine what kind of ticket I get and how much it will cost.

The NLP label for the process of moving up or down the ladder of abstraction is *chunking*. When we chunk *up* we start with the details ('specifics') and work up to the overview. Chunking *down* means breaking down an 'abstract' overview into ever more precise details.

In a business context, people who prefer to deal in specifics tend to be 'backroom boys'. They seldom rise very high on the management scale because they don't feel comfortable dealing with 'big picture' thinking, which can seem unnecessarily vague and impractical – which of course it is, since dealing in big chunks takes you into the area of 'what' is to be done rather than 'how' it is to be done.

Those who rise highest on the corporate ladder, even though they may have started out acquiring specific skills, usually have the ability to take in, and make decisions from, the 'big picture' perspective, without getting caught up in the details.

Plus or minus two

According to one famous study, by psychologist George Miller, human beings can only consciously deal with seven 'chunks' of information, plus or minus two, at any given moment. That is to say, we can only hold 7 ± 2 chunks of information in what Miller called 'immediate memory', which is now more usually referred to as 'working' or 'short-term' memory, at any one time. But just how much information is there in a 'chunk'?

As Miller himself explained, the simple answer is that there is no simple answer: 'the number of chunks of information is constant for immediate memory. The span of immediate memory seems to be almost independent of the number of bits per chunk, at least over the range that has been examined to date.'

In practice, chunk size varies from person to person, and even from topic to topic. It also tends to grow in size as you become more familiar with the material. Just consider the following 'explanation':

> For VAT purposes, cross debit incomings and outgoings and enter the transaction in the day book and the residue in the bought ledger, unless the rolling annual total becomes negative, in which case record the transaction as an inverse credit payment, and enter the balance on an F11/789/K.

To the average person this paragraph contains at least eight chunks of information and probably looks quite genuine. An experienced bookkeeper, however, will probably see at a glance that the whole thing is sheer nonsense.

Picking the right level

Selecting the correct chunk size in a given situation, and knowing whether to chunk up or down – or both – are key skills in interpersonal communication.
No matter what the situation, if you chunk correctly you will have a significantly better chance of getting your message across. Choose the wrong chunk size, or chunk in the wrong direction, and you might as well stay at home.

Abstract mode

Someone in this mode is only interested in the big picture. Get too detailed and the *abstract* mode listener begins to switch off. If you really *must* go into details, then keep them as few and simple as possible, and make sure that you present them in an interesting or amusing way.

Abstract to specific mode

This group needs the overview first in order to have a framework on which to hang the details which follow. Although they are willing to deal with a certain amount of detail, they have an instinctive feel (not necessarily infallible) for how much detail they need about a given subject. Once you cross this boundary – if you start to get *too* specific – then they are also likely to simply tune you out.

Specific mode

'But I did exactly what you asked. How was I to know the information was for a customer?' is typical of the sort of complaint made by someone in *specific* mode. They may be excellent at their particular job, but may find it difficult to relate what they do to the business of the department or company as a whole.

When taking on new information/skills people in *specific* mode like to have plenty of details, preferably with the underlying theory and some basic hands-on experience. Indeed, they may never feel ready to actually use a new skill until their knowledge is positively encyclopaedic (which is never, of course).

Specific to abstract mode

This is the most practical of the four modes we've looked at. A person in this mode does need to get some detailed information in front of them when approaching a new activity, learning a new skill or whatever, but they are at least willing to build on that information to work towards a synergistic understanding (that is, a view that is greater than the mere sum of the details).

People who prefer this mode are often seen as the backbone of a company. They're happy to do what they do day in and day out with commendable consistency, yet are capable of flashes of unexpected creativity if they are given the right encouragement – or even just because one little detail suddenly falls into place.

Why middle managers matter

Whilst senior managers and sales people mostly work at 'big chunk' level, the day-to-day operations of any business function mainly at the 'small chunk' level. One of the key functions of an effective middle manager is to mediate between the two extremes, and companies which 'de-layer' too enthusiastically often find that they are left with a serious communications gap.

Even with the appropriate layer(s) of middle management in place, however, it is still important to ensure that *all* members of management maintain a degree of flexibility, or else something like this may happen:

Jim Binnet was 'a man with a plan' when he joined Sonata Systems as a project manager. In fact he saw nearly everything about his job in the sort of 'big picture' perspective that is more usually associated with a much more senior level of management. Indeed, though he never looked closely enough at his own behaviour to see it, his outlook, with its consequent failure to take care of details, put Jim's projects, and his job, at risk. Initially he was protected from this fate by his two senior team leaders, who frequently found themselves having to carry out work that was rightfully Jim's own responsibility.

Typical of Jim's attitude was his behaviour in meetings, where he learnt to conceal his boredom when the discussion got too detailed by staring enigmatically into the distance until someone finished speaking. Then Jim would fix the speaker with an unwavering stare and ask a question such as 'Is that definite?' or 'Are you certain about that?' This allowed Jim to appear incisive even when he hadn't the faintest idea what had just been said. (After all, he could always check his secretary's notes if he really needed to know what had been going on!)

Of course this didn't all happen out of a clear blue sky. Jim's attitude and behaviour were actually looked upon most favourably by two of the directors of the company, both of whom lived in a similarly rarefied atmosphere where 'vision' was everything and 'taking care of business' was something one left to one's underlings.

In other words, Jim, the 'big chunker', was being championed by two people who were chunking on an even grander scale.

Over a relatively short period of time, and much to the puzzlement of other members of the company who had a pretty accurate view of Jim's abilities – but little or no understanding of the material covered in this book – Jim rose to senior management level. Moreover, he was frequently put in charge of headline-grabbing initiatives such as the 'External Relations Project', designed to reverse the company's failure to hang on to many of its best customers. Naturally these programmes never achieved very much, given Jim's comprehensive inattention to detail, but even that didn't impede his progress, for the simple reason that the two directors whom Jim was working to had an even shorter attention span and frequently cancelled these projects and moved Jim on to something else before the full extent of his failure to deliver could be assessed.

Clearly, then, when going through the process of evaluating someone's skills, whether it be for the purposes of recruitment or for promotion, it is important to assess whether that person is able to adjust their preferred information chunk size to the needs of each situation or whether they favour a 'one size fits all' approach – especially if that 'one size' attitude is likely to be inappropriate to the role they are required to fill.

Checkpoint actions

1. Check whether it's true that people usually chunk the information they give to other people using about the same chunk size that they would prefer when someone else is giving them information.
   a. When someone is giving you information, gauge how vague or precise they are being.
   b. Offer to check the information back to them, but when you do so be more precise or more vague.
   c. Does the other person correct you? Do the corrections mirror the chunk size they used before?
2. Select a topic on a subject you know well. Imagine that you are going to discuss this topic with two groups of people:
   a. Group A are familiar with the subject but not the topic.
   b. Group B have no relevant background knowledge of any kind.
   Break down the topic into 'chunks' suitable for each group and decide, in each case, whether you need to chunk up or chunk down for best effect.

14

What do you think?

I wonder...

Three important facets of NLP are:

1. asking questions;
2. knowing the right questions to ask; and
3. knowing when and how to ask them.

Generally speaking, the purpose of asking a question, in the context of NLP, is either to get information or to get the person who is being asked the question to think about the answer.

The facts, ma'am, just the facts

The idea of asking questions to get information may seem rather obvious, until we look at it a little more carefully.

First of all, if we're asking for information that implies that this is something we don't yet have. But just because we don't have a particular piece of information doesn't automatically mean that we actually need it. Remember the example of the trip to London, in the last chapter. The point we were making was that the significance of a phrase like 'I'm going to London' was dependent on the context in which it occurred. If it was said by someone wanting to purchase a railway ticket for the journey then the ticket clerk would need some further clarification as to whether the traveller wanted to use a first class or a second class compartment, whether they wanted a single or a return, and so on. If the comment was made in passing during a conversation between friends or acquaintances, however, then the listener would be more likely to ask about the purpose of the trip (which would most likely be irrelevant to the ticket clerk), or they might simply take the statement at face value and not feel the need to ask any questions at all.

The point to be considered, then, is not simply 'Is there any information missing from what I am being told?' but rather 'Is there any information missing which I actually *need to know* (for whatever reason), and, if so, what *specifically* do I need to know that I haven't been told/shown so far?'

The meta model

According to most authoritative accounts, the meta model was the earliest model created during the development of NLP. It is a linguistic model, largely based on Noam Chomsky's ideas on *Transformational Grammar* (John Grinder's particular field of interest and one on which he had co-authored a book in the period leading up to his collaboration with Richard Bandler).

In NLP jargon, linguistically ill-formed sentences are referred to as 'meta model violations'. To be more precise, the meta model is actually a list of linguistic structures which are said to be *ill* formed, and 'meta model violations' are not phrases which *violate* the meta model but the linguistic structures listed *in* the meta model. The basic underlying concept is that the words we use to create grammatically correct phrases and sentences (*surface structures*) only partially reflect the speaker or writer's underlying thoughts (*deep structures*).

In total, the meta model lists a dozen generic structures which appear meaningful but which actually conceal what the speaker is really thinking. Indeed, even the speaker may not realise what they are doing by using these structures. So when we ask the appropriate meta model question, we not only gain useful information; we may also help the speaker to consider the full implications of what they are saying. Five of the most commonly used meta model violations are:

▪ **Comparisons.** The speaker makes a comparison but leaves out the basis for the comparison (a favourite advertising ploy). For example: 'This is the best laptop computer on the market.' To evaluate this claim we need to know 'Which market?' and 'By what yardstick is it "best"? On price, features, battery life per charge, or what?'

▪ **Universal quantifiers.** The speaker makes a sweeping generalisation, as in: 'The paperwork is never completed on time!' Since it is very unusual for anything to be *always* right, or *never* right, and so on, we need to ask the speaker if their generalisation really is universally applicable, as in: 'The paperwork has *never* been completed on time, not even once?'

▪ **Unquestioned rules.** The speaker cites the necessity to conform to a rule for which there is no better justification than something like: 'That's the way we've always done it.' Rather than question the rule itself we might ask questions designed to open up new possibilities, like: 'What other ways could this be done?' and 'What would happen if you did it another way?'

▪ **Unspecified nouns.** The speaker recounts an event using 'high level' descriptions instead of specific details, such as: 'Someone hurt themselves in the machine shop.' This is hardly adequate for the health and safety record, and we need to ask: 'Who hurt themselves? Give me their name.'

▪ **Unspecified verbs.** The speaker recounts an event using a 'high level' verb, or verbs, instead of identifying specific actions. Using the previous example we also need to ask: 'How did this person hurt themselves? What did they actually do?'

The full list of meta model violations also includes:

■ **Cause and effect.** The speaker describes two events – A and B – as though event B is *caused* by event A. 'It makes me so angry when you are late.' (How does someone's behaviour control the speaker's emotions?)

■ **Complex equivalence.** The speaker names two separate items and treats them as though they were the same thing. 'You didn't phone. What have I done wrong?' (How does not phoning imply that you've done anything wrong?)

■ **Lack of referential index.** The speaker uses a pronoun instead of a name or title so that it is not clear who or what the speaker is talking about, for example the ubiquitous 'they', as in: 'They won't like it.' (Who are 'they'? What is 'it'?)

■ **Lost performative.** The speaker delivers some kind of judgement without identifying the source. 'People should only express their opinions if they are well informed.' (Who says so?)

■ **Mind reading.** The speaker assumes that whatever they think they know about what another person is thinking or feeling must be true: 'You want to make me look bad in front of the boss.' (What gave you that idea?)

■ **Modal operator.** A word which implies an unspecified rule, such as: 'I *should* do abc' (modal operator of *necessity*), or which implies options, or a lack of options, such as: 'I *can't* do that' (modal operator of *possibility*).

■ **Nominalisation.** The speaker refers to a process as though it were a static event, for example: 'Our relationship with this customer is not very good.' (Which aspect(s) of the *interaction* between you and this particular customer are not satisfactory?)

■ **Presupposition.** The speaker says something that assumes that a second, unspoken, statement is true when in fact it may *or may not* be true. For example: 'Don't cause any more trouble.' (Implies that the person *has* caused trouble at some time in the past.)

■ **Simple deletion.** The speaker uses a sentence that is grammatically correct but omits some essential information, as in: 'Things have really started to improve!' (What, in particular, do you think has started to improve?)

Be gentle with me

When the meta model was first being developed, Bandler and Grinder found that their students were encountering considerable resistance when they asked the meta model questions straight out (as shown above), because they sounded more like an interrogation than simple requests for information.

It is better to couch the questions in a way that softens that interrogatory edge, as in:

■ For mind reading: 'It's interesting you should say that. Was there anything in particular that gave you that idea?'
■ For simple deletion: 'What would you say has improved the most?'

Telling without telling

The notion of asking someone a question in order to *tell* them something may seem a trifle bizarre, yet we actually do it quite regularly. That is to say, we ask a question in order to trigger an idea rather than because we want to hear the answer. And we can do it directly or indirectly. For example, lawyers really do ask witnesses questions which they know in advance will not get answered (a 'leading question', for example) and which, in all likelihood, the judge will order the jury to disregard. So why do they do it? They ask such questions because it allows them to put the relevant thought into the minds of the jury members – who, in most cases, will *not* disregard the question and may actually take *more* notice than if nothing had been said about it.

Moreover, making the point in the form of a question is often a much more effective way of planting ideas, or drawing out the other person's thoughts, than making a direct statement. In part this is because a question is, by definition, normally part of an interaction. The flow of the exchange is expected to pause until you have answered my question, or I have answered yours, as the case may be. A statement, on the other hand, doesn't *need* any response to make it complete. Then again, a question, asked in a reasonable manner, is like a request, whereas even a perfectly innocuous statement can seem confrontational. The one draws out the listener's own view, whilst the other may seem to be telling the listener what they should think.

Checkpoint action

For best results: 'Practise (listening for evidence of missing information), Practise (deciding whether what's missing really matters), Practise (framing suitable questions to retrieve the missing information in a respectful manner).'

15

Avoiding resistance

I wanna tell you a story

Once upon a time a certain man, an architect by profession, was asked by a friend to draw up plans for a modest town house.

'I've bought some land, and although I have no experience, I'm sure it can't be hard to build your own house. After all, if it were hard, there wouldn't be so many of them, would there?'

The architect, realising that his friend would not allow himself to be argued out of his intention, worked on the plans as requested, taking special care to make them as comprehensive and easy to follow as he possibly could.

About two weeks later the architect went down to the building site to see how things were getting on. He was amazed to find his friend standing beside a large stack of new bricks, with a mound of broken bricks on his other side.

He was even more amazed to see his friend take a brick from the pile on his left and hit it with a hammer, then toss the pieces on to the mound of broken bricks on his right.

'What on earth are you doing?' asked the architect, 'You're destroying perfectly good bricks treating them like that.'

'Perfectly good bricks?' said the friend, 'I don't think so. See how easily they break. The bricks with which I build my house will have to support a structure that weighs tons. I need to know whether the materials are good enough to do the job!'

The heart of the matter

Pierre Casse, a professor at the International Institute for Management Development in Lausanne, says, regarding the use of metaphors: 'When you hear a negotiator say, "*Oh, that reminds me of a story...*" – be alert – at once... a **story** is always dangerous in the sense that it is a **metaphor...**'

A metaphor, as Professor Casse explains, works on at least two levels. On the conscious level it is simply what it appears to be – an anecdote or fable. On the second level it allows us to talk to the subconscious mind in such a way that the conscious mind cannot censor or reject the underlying message(s).

In the story at the start of this chapter, for example, the overt message is a mild kind of joke.

But at a deeper level, the story has several messages, including:

■ Even an expert can't necessarily prevent a friend from making a fool of himself.
■ Don't assume that a job is easy just because it's been done many times before.
■ Logic becomes counterproductive when applied in an illogical manner.

One word of warning before we move on: Because metaphors always carry indirect messages, anyone who hears the story, even if it was not meant for them, may hear a deeper meaning which you, the story teller, had never thought of or intended.

War is hell

You don't have to tell a whole story in order to use metaphors, of course. 'Time is money', 'a dog-eat-dog world', 'a cut-throat business' – these are all very meaningful metaphors of the type we hear around us every day. But how often do we stop to consider the consequences of using a particular set of metaphors?

How flexible can you be if you go into a negotiating session with the attitude 'We take no prisoners'? It doesn't mesh with seeking win/win solutions, and is more likely to result in some major wins and some equally major losses, with not much in between.

Internationally renowned NLP trainer Lara Ewing tells the story of a group of managers who were looking for appropriate metaphors to illustrate their individual roles within the company. As they went round the group one man introduced himself as 'The company fire-fighter'. The description sounded innocent enough at the time, but when the seminar was over another manager explained to Lara that the 'fire-fighter' included a metaphorical box of matches amongst his equipment. So if the gap between 'fires' seemed to be getting too long, the fire-fighter was liable to start one of his own in order to justify his existence!

Checkpoint actions

1. Watch how frequently people explain themselves with little stories. How does this affect your own understanding of what (you think) they are trying to say?
2. Use story-telling to enliven your own conversation, remembering that, in the business context, *short* stories work best.
3. What metaphors would you use to describe your company, the way it operates, and your main role within the company?
4. Listen out for the metaphors that your colleagues use in the work context. How accurate do you think they are?

16

Self-management

Do you mean what you say?

It may be hard to comprehend just how little effect what we *say* may have if it does not convey the same message given out by our vocal characteristics (tone, tempo, variability, etc) and our body language. If these three factors are not in accord – if we are not *congruent* – people will weigh up the message that they receive from each of the three forms of communication. (See FAQ 17 on my website at http://www.bradburyac.mistral.co.uk for a more detailed explanation.)

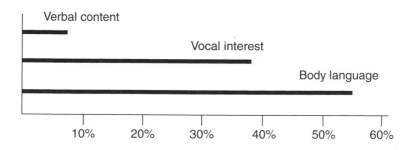

These figures show why we need to understand and manage our own *non-verbal* cues if we want our messages to be heard and *accurately* understood.

Values and beliefs

True congruence only occurs when we are behaving in complete accordance with our beliefs and values, working to a clear-cut and well-focused outcome, and when our words, vocal signals and body language are naturally synchronised.

Admittedly, much of life consists of making compromises, and achieving complete congruence is something of a struggle.

One way of achieving congruence is to push everything else to one side. Like a top-class athlete we can become so focused on the job in hand that nothing else intrudes upon our thoughts to distract us from achieving a particular outcome.

The strategy does have its limitations, however. Applied for short periods it can be extremely effective, but if we make this our primary behaviour pattern over a protracted period of time we are likely to become – in other people's view – not congruent but 'obsessive', 'blinkered' and afflicted with 'tunnel vision'.

Congruence is a source of tremendous sustainable power, in the context of achieving outcomes. It is a way of being highly focused without becoming cold, ruthless or any of the other negative qualities we normally associate with an out-and-out go-getter. The solution is to maintain, as far as possible, an integrated posture by getting all of your *parts* to act in harmony.

A typical example of *incongruence* in the workplace is the person who values the social perks of belonging to a team, but also wants to be valued as an individual. Adept team leaders and managers ensure that their people get that recognition without having to act in a way which could disrupt the smooth running of the team.

The sum of the parts

Have you ever said something like: 'I think I agree, but part of me still isn't convinced'? According to NLP, when you talk this way – '*part* of me', 'I'm a *bit* worried', 'I'm not *entirely* sure' – it is something more than a mere figure of speech.

The 'bit' or 'part' is some portion of your subconscious which carries out a particular action or otherwise serves (or has served) some useful purpose. A typical 'part' is the 'little critic', the internal voice that serves a useful purpose by guiding us away from making careless mistakes, but which can also eat away at our self-confidence if it is constantly carping.

These parts are what we deal with in the *programming* aspect of NLP, and getting all of your parts to work together is the basis of a congruent posture. The more unanimity there is between the parts – the more congruent you are – the greater the potential for effective action.

Talking to parts

Imagine what it might be like to have a fear of heights. One part of you might say: 'I want to go to the 15th floor of this building to attend an important meeting', but if another part says: 'No way, that's much too high – I'm not going up there!', there is a distinct chance that you won't get to the meeting.

To achieve congruence you might do a deal with the part that is afraid of heights, such as: 'I'll go to the 15th floor but I won't watch the floor indicator in the lift, I won't look out of the windows, and I'll come back down as soon as I can.'

This is not to say that it is necessary to believe that your *self* is literally divided into hundreds of separate 'parts'. Like much of NLP, the concept of parts is simply a metaphor designed to convey an idea which works *as if* it were literally true.

It is possible, however, to have conversations with your 'parts', as the 'fear of heights' example suggested, and this can be very effective in a range of business situations.

The essential point is to recognise that the tensions that arise within us when we approach an important, new or emotionally charged experience (or any other experience, for that matter) are perfectly natural. The real question is: will we try to struggle through without resolving the tension – in a state of *in*congruence – or will we 're-program' our response to achieve a more harmonious, congruent and effective state?

Andrew Carnegie, self-made multi-millionaire and philanthropist, would often break off in the middle of a business meeting and go into another office by himself whilst he talked through the progress of the meeting, playing out the actions of everyone involved. Only when he was clear about his own position – his own outcome – would he rejoin the meeting.

> Never negotiate with yourself in front of your competitors.

Incidentally, we are naturally quite adept at recognising significant states of congruence or incongruence in other people. The phrase: 'I don't know why, he just made me feel uncomfortable' is a typical expression of this instinctive awareness.

'Need-to-know' management

A topic closely related to congruence is the practice of 'need-to-know'-style management: 'If you need to know, I'll tell you; if I don't tell you then you don't need to know.'

Of course, it is the right of management to release information 'at their own discretion'. But if it is impossible to know *everything* about even the simplest situation, how can we ever know in advance exactly what people will *need to know*? So, is a need-to-know policy really congruent with effective management and encouraging employees to act like responsible adults? Probably not.

Checkpoint action

We all talk to our 'parts' at some time or other, and these internal dialogues are perfectly natural. So get into the habit of listening to your inner voice. Learn to take advantage of your 'hidden depths', and take control of the 'little critic'.

17

Using preferred thinking styles

Find the pattern

The discussion of the five representational systems in Chapter 5 was mainly concerned with how to identify which sense or senses were being given priority at any given time. But simply knowing whether a person is thinking in pictures, or sounds, or feelings, etc, isn't a lot of use unless we can put that knowledge to good use. In this chapter we will deal with the three most frequently used rep systems – how to identify which system a person is using and how to use that information to improve the effectiveness of our communications.

By the way, if you haven't already read Chapter 5, that's where you'll find details of the eye positions and sample predicates for each of the three most popular representational systems.

Visual mode

When someone is in visual mode they will tend to think, talk and behave as though their entire mental processes are held on film. They are likely to talk quite fast, and may be impatient when interrupted because they need to talk as fast as the film show running in their head. An interruption may literally cause them to lose a part of that picture. At best, they may be able to re-run the film and pick up at the point where they were interrupted. At worst, that part of their thoughts may be lost entirely.

Being in visual mode is also characterised by a higher-than-average amount of physical movement – such as hand gestures to complement whatever is being said, pacing the floor whilst talking, and looking around at anything other than the person they are speaking to. This does not indicate a lack of respect or interest. They are simply trying to avoid anything which might distract them from that internal film show.

Some advantages of the visual mode thinking include the ability to 'see' the big picture yet just as easily zoom in on a specific detail, and a greater ability to 'think on one's feet', as compared to someone in auditory or kinaesthetic mode.

The main disadvantages are an over-dependence on visual information, low tolerance of interruptions, and difficulty in dealing with any kind of information which cannot readily be represented in graphical form such as lists, or sets of figures.

Persuasion

When you hear a manager saying something like 'It's not what you do, it's what you look like you're doing' or 'It's people's perceptions that count', you're probably listening to someone who is in visual mode. The problem is that you can't *see* someone thinking. This can lead to the (quite possibly erroneous) assumption that the person who is always hustling round with a fistful of papers is doing more work than someone who is relatively static because whatever task the latter person is engaged in takes a great deal of thought.

Taken to extremes, a manager who spends much of her time in visual mode can so demotivate the people doing the real work that she ends up with a department full of paper shufflers, at the same time believing that she has swept the office clean of time wasters!

So if you tend to favour visual mode, remember that we usually see what we expect to see. If you want to hang on to your best staff, take notice of who actually produces results, rather than who simply *looks* busy.

In order to impress a manager who is in visual mode, find ways to show her what you have achieved. Don't waste time just *telling* her what you've been doing, because unless you can back your words up with something visual all that you say will go in one ear and out the other.

By the same token, when giving instructions to someone who favours visual mode thinking, you will need to literally show them what you want them to do. This can be by showing them an example of what they have to produce, giving a demonstration of the process they must follow, and so on.

Auditory mode

Is there anyone in your company who often talks to themselves, especially when they are concentrating really hard? If so, it is very likely that they spend quite a lot of their time in auditory mode, which is when we interact with the world around us primarily through sounds, and especially through words.

People who feel comfortable in auditory mode play an important part in the life of the companies where they work, because it is in auditory mode that we function best at tasks that require 'live' communication, be it face to face, on the telephone, and so on. Like a kind of human 'voice analyser', someone in auditory mode will be sensitive to both *what* is said and *how* it is said – tone of voice, etc – though they may not realise that they have this skill.

The main drawback of being in auditory mode is that we may find that we are easily distracted by loud or disharmonious noises. (Creating an auditorially soothing background in the workplace can reduce absenteeism and raise productivity by as much as 18 and 22 per cent respectively.) For this reason someone who favours auditory mode may prefer to get to work early, or stay on late, in order to have some time when they can work without being disturbed.

On the other hand, some people, when in auditory mode, tend to be somewhat assertive, even domineering, in meetings and even in simple conversations. This is because they need to verbalise their thoughts in order to clarify their own ideas.

Persuasion

When dealing with a manager in auditory mode, the best course is to present your information or request as succinctly as possible, in verbal form, and then leave her to make a decision.

Use a vocal style that is varied and interesting, remembering that auditory mode often includes an element of internal dialogue. If you require clarification, ask questions rather than making statements, and use questions that begin with 'What' rather than 'Why'.

Strange as it may seem to people who prefer visual or kinaesthetic mode as their main thinking style, someone in auditory mode may not know exactly what they want you to do until they hear themselves say it out loud. This may mean that they run through the details more than once as they sort things out in their own mind, so leave your comments or questions till they have clearly finished their message.

Giving instructions and information to someone in auditory mode is best done verbally, at a tempo roughly equivalent to their own normal rate of speech and by someone with an interesting voice. They are more likely to ask questions and come back for verbal clarification after a presentation or after having been assigned a task. This is nothing more than the auditory mode equivalent of reading written instructions through a couple of times before starting to carry them out.

Having said that, someone in auditory mode might actually appreciate a 'need-to-know' policy (Chapter 16). In auditory mode we make decisions very largely on the basis of what we *hear*, or more precisely: on what we can *remember* of what we have heard. When we are in visual or kinaesthetic mode, we may find it valuable to store information in hard copy format (and review it at our leisure). In auditory mode, however, we are likely to find it much easier to sort and review whatever information we've been given inside our heads. This is obviously a great deal easier if the information is kept to the appropriate minimum.

Kinaesthetic mode

The word 'kinaesthetic' comes from the Greek words *kinein* (to move) and *aisthesthai* (to perceive), and is commonly used to refer to the physical sense of movement. In NLP the word is used to refer to 'feelings' in general, both tactile and emotional. The style of speech associated with the kinaesthetic mode tends to be slower than average (allowing the speaker time to make frequent internal checks on their feelings).

More than any other time, being in kinaesthetic mode may lead us to attach great importance to our feelings (especially our emotions). But emotions have no content, and tend to be somewhat transitory, which often makes it difficult to deal with logical reasoning until we have decided how we feel about the topic in question.

A person in kinaesthetic mode who is primarily attuned to their own feelings can appear to be rather introverted and insensitive, even 'cold'. Someone who is in kinaesthetic mode and externally focused, on the other hand, will be much more attuned to the people and events around them, and they are likely to feel particularly unsettled and vulnerable if their circumstances become emotionally charged or physically chaotic, for whatever reason.

On this basis, it is usually not a good idea to go into kinaesthetic mode when you are required to deal with high-pressure situations, as you need time to interpret incoming information in relation to previous experiences and emotions. Having said that, a person who has learnt how to balance the internal and external aspects of the kinaesthetic mode can often achieve considerable success in business, especially in areas which demand a high degree of empathy, such as negotiating and personnel functions.

Persuasion

In kinaesthetic mode we tend to attach very little importance to visual and auditory information, preferring to rely on our 'gut reactions'. This can lead to notable successes, or equally notable fiascos if we miss the mark.

Having reached a decision, a person in kinaesthetic mode may find it difficult to change their mind, even when contrary evidence is placed before them. To get someone in kinaesthetic mode to take notice you will need to reach them at an emotional level, a task which is most easily achieved through the use of metaphors (Chapter 15). Do remember, however, that the listener will not necessarily receive exactly the same message that you intended.

When we're in kinaesthetic mode, we tend to prioritise our work according to our personal feelings about each task. It is therefore helpful to give each task emotional weighting when we're talking to someone in this mode. For example: 'I'd appreciate it if you'd give this matter top priority' or 'I don't mind when you do this, as long as you have it finished by the end of the week.'

In fact, when we are in kinaesthetic mode we need an emotional framework around everything that we do. To this end we are liable to build internal versions of the feelings of the people around us – which we then interpret as fact. It is not unusual to come across 'middle-order' managers who claim to understand senior management's innermost thoughts – and insist that everyone behave according to this 'knowledge'. Sometimes this may be a case of trying to gain authority by claiming close association with someone further up the corporate ladder.

On the other hand, this is quite typical behaviour for a kinaesthetic mode 'mind reader', who may be doing it out of a genuine belief that they have this special ability to understand the wishes of the more senior manager or managers. For what it's worth, no amount of rational explanation will get them to think differently.

18

Presentations

Who are you talking to?

One of the worst, and most common, mistakes made by presenters is to assume that the most important element in a 'good' presentation is a well-constructed argument. Wrong! The best foundation for *any* presentation is to establish and maintain rapport with your audience. Like every other aspect of communication, what happens at the non-verbal level is often far more important to the success of a presentation than any amount of clever scripting.

In a superficial sense, presentations come in all shapes and sizes, from a one-to-one training session up to a major bells and whistles and coloured lights multimedia event. To some extent, then, the way you handle a particular presentation – what visual aids you use, and so on – should reflect the size and purpose of the event. But that, too, is secondary to the job of creating the bond between the audience and yourself.

The following list shows five elements which are applicable to *any* presentation, which form the rather appropriate mnemonic OSCAR:

clear	Outcome
layered	Structure
selective	Chunking
positive	Attitude
flexible	Response

Outcome

No presentation is going to be successful if it doesn't have a clearly defined outcome, or set of outcomes – at least one for you and one for your audience (Chapter 6). For example:

▪ I want to give a brief and powerful presentation of three key reasons why my new product idea should be accepted for manufacture.

▪ I want the people at the presentation to support my proposal and feed in any ideas they may have for improvements.

These outcomes should be clearly detailed at the start of the event, and adhered to: 'I'm going to describe three key reasons why this product should go into production. In addition to the details I'm going to set out for you, I'm really interested in getting any ideas you may have for improving on the basic specification.'

This approach quickly puts the audience at ease because they no longer have the feeling that they must blindly follow wherever you choose to lead. It also provides a framework which will make it easier for your audience to understand and remember the points made during the presentation.

Structure

In order to effectively utilise preferred thinking styles (Chapters 5 and 17) and meta programs (Chapters 12 and 13), take extra care over the *structure* of your presentation. Make sure that you switch frequently, but not obviously, from one PTS to another throughout the presentation. And take care to cater to whichever meta programs you think are relevant (towards–away from, sameness–difference, etc). By addressing appropriate meta programs you are telling people in the most direct way possible: 'This is for *you*!'

Chunking

Also on the subject of meta programs, be sure to 'chunk' your material (Chapter 13) so as to retain audience interest.

Since individual members of your audience will have different preferences, your best option is to choose a middle-of-the-range starting point, and then chunk up. Allow questions from the audience so that people can ask for more detail if they wish, but avoid getting bogged down in 'nitty-gritty' details (unless that level of detail is a necessary element of the event).

Attitude

This means more than simply 'think positive'. Effective presenters share an unusually high level of self-confidence, at least whilst they are delivering a presentation. It is as though they will the event to succeed by their unflagging belief in that success, a belief that will be conveyed to and impressed upon the audience through a variety of non-verbal signals.

Response

There are at least three positions from which you can view any situation – your own, the other person's standpoint, and that of an impartial observer. In NLP these are known as first, second and third position, respectively.

The fifth quality that contributes to a truly impressive presentation style is a mixture of sensitivity and flexibility. Top presenters constantly switch back and forth between viewpoints, always aware of the response they are getting from their audience, and able to customise the presentation as they go in order to achieve their desired outcome.

'Anchoring the room'

A question that comes up regularly in presentation skills courses is: 'Should I move about and, if so, how much?'

In practice this isn't quite the right question. For someone who feels comfortable staying relatively still, it would be a mistake to start pacing around 'because they should'. And for someone who feels comfortable moving around, it would be equally wrong to restrict their movements too much.

A more useful consideration is how moving around during a presentation – by 'anchoring the room' – can be used to good effect.

In brief, this technique is based on the idea that if we repeat certain actions in a consistent manner then we can use the actions as non-verbal signals to give the presentation an additional structure.

As a simple example, suppose I consistently move between three positions – stage left, centre stage and stage right. And suppose I only move to one of those positions when I come to particular points in my presentation. When I have an important fact to convey I move to the left side of the stage. When I'm presenting less important linking material I go to stage centre. And on the occasions when I want to be light-hearted I position myself on the right-hand side of the stage.

After I've done this a few times most members of the audience will understand, though probably unconsciously, what it signifies when I move to one or another of the three positions and will be more in tune with my message as a consequence.

19

Modelling

What one person *can* do, other people can *learn* to do

One of the core activities in NLP is the study of people who are recognised (by their peers) as being excellent in some field of activity. The purpose of this studying is to identify what such people do differently from their colleagues which gives them such outstanding results. This is often referred to as 'the difference that makes the difference'.

When the differences have been identified they can then be communicated to other people who can learn to perform the same activity with a similar level of skill and excellence. In this regard we might recall the presupposition that *context makes meaning*, and the best results are likely to come from modelling as closely as possible to the context in which the results of the modelling will be used.

Having said that, the person *learning* the skill must have the necessary aptitude, *and* be willing to carry out the necessary self-development. In other words, whilst it is easy enough to study, or *model*, the activity of a world-class sprinter, for example, a person who has only one leg, or is severely over-weight, or who refuses to take any physical exercise, is unlikely to be able to translate the modelled information into a personal skill.

NLP is modelling is NLP

So important is the skill of modelling, in NLP, that it has been said that NLP *is* modelling, and that all the techniques and methodology that most people think of as NLP are actually just tools designed to facilitate the modelling process. Not surprisingly, then, modelling is the most complex aspect of NLP, and the one which is most obviously still evolving.

Modelling can be extremely useful in the business context, especially in terms of disseminating proven skills. For example, if one manager consistently brings in projects on time and within budget, then rather than sending other managers off on some generic course, it may be more effective to model that manager and pass the results on to other members of the management team. Assuming that experts are brought in to do the modelling and course design, this may initially appear to be the more expensive option. But as the relevant knowledge and skills are passed on, and practical results are generated – fewer budget and deadline overruns, leading to more satisfied customers and thus to more repeat business – the cost should be far outweighed by improvements to the bottom line of the balance sheet, and within a reasonably short period of time.

We will not be discussing modelling in any great detail in this book, for the simple reason that it is a subject which requires a book all on its own to do it justice. There are, however, certain guidelines which are worth setting down.

Types of modelling

There are, in fact, two types of modelling used in NLP: *observational* modelling; and *adoptive* modelling. Moreover, the first type of modelling is more accurately described as a category, since there are in fact two types of observational modelling used in NLP.

Observational modelling

What I mean by 'observational modelling' is creating a model of another person by copying them in some way. The two types of observational modelling are:

Additive modelling

This is probably what most people in NLP think of in connection with modelling. It basically involves:

1. deciding on a skill you would like to have;
2. finding an exemplar – someone who already has the skill you want;
3. identifying the factors which appear to support that skill in the exemplar;
4. (optional) capturing, or codifying, those factors in such a form that they can be passed on to other people who wish to share that skill.

Subtractive modelling

When Richard Bandler first started to replicate the work of gestalt therapist Fritz Perls, he did so in a very complete way. Not only did he use Perls' particular approach to therapy – he reproduced Perls' heavily Germanic accent, his smoking habits and everything else that he'd heard and seen on the tapes he was transcribing. It was as though Bandler was matching Perls' skill as a therapist – and achieving comparable results – by becoming Perls. But was this kind of total immersion actually necessary? Do we need to become a virtual clone of the person we're modelling in order to take on a particular skill? In a nutshell, no we don't, as Bandler and Grinder discovered when they formalised their process of *subtractive modelling*.

In this approach the modeller will:

1. Initially take on aspects of the subject's behaviour – actions, attitudes, etc – which they can observe and/or elicit, making

no judgements or evaluations as to the relevance or usefulness of any particular feature.

2. Test whether they can now achieve results similar to those obtained by the subject. If they can then they move on to Step 3; otherwise they return to Step 1.

3. Identify all of the individual features of the subject that the modeller thinks they have adopted. A list of these features will be drawn up – still without making any judgements about the comparative value of each feature.

4. Start to carry out whatever relevant activities the subject performs (selling a house, running 800 metres, carrying out an exit interview, or whatever). On each occasion, however, the modeller will discard one of their listed features and note what difference this makes to their results. If there doesn't seem to be any significant difference, or if there is a change because results improve, that feature stays discarded. If the results are noticeably poorer then the feature is reinstated.

5. Repeat Step 4 until all definable features have been tested (giving due consideration to the fact that some features may be 'interactive', such as voice tone and a particular form of wording, so that neither has much effect on its own, but they become very powerful when used in combination).

6. Whatever is left after completing Step 5 should be the minimum set of features needed to gain the required results.

The techniques that became the *applications* of NLP were mainly developed by Bandler and Grinder using this subtractive style of modelling. It should be clear, from the description above, that this is a fairly complex technique and not one that is suitable for use where a 'quick fix' or 'cheap and dirty' solution is required. By the same token, however, when the process is used efficiently it should produce far more useful, and cost-effective, results than a less rigorous approach would deliver.

Adoptive modelling

Once a skill or ability has been modelled in the observational sense, it must then be described in such a way that it can be taught to other people who do not have that skill, or who have it but to a lesser extent. In other words, it must be presented in such a way that people can integrate the model into their own behaviour patterns. This obviously calls for quite a lot of information, but it must be a sufficient amount of the right information. On this basis it often helps if the people who will be adopting the model understand some of the subtleties of producing a viable model. For example:

▨ One of the identifying characteristics of a true 'expert' is that they exercise their expertise unconsciously – without having to think about it (Chapter 2). As a consequence...

▨ Asking an expert to identify their key skills and techniques is usually a waste of time, because...

▨ Most experts worth modelling either don't know what they do that makes them 'expert' or identify the wrong elements of their behaviour as being the basis of their success.

▨ So, an inflexible, legalistic use of a model – simply *consciously* mimicking an expert's behaviour – may not produce much in the way of results. The model must be integrated at the unconscious level so that the behaviour becomes as natural as the model user's own behaviour.

▨ Effective modelling must take account of three aspects of the subject being modelled:
  – **behaviour:** what the expert does;
  – **beliefs:** the 'mental maps' (Chapter 3) that are the foundation for this behaviour;
  – **values:** the criteria by which the expert decides on any particular course of action.

▨ In addition to whatever specific behaviour you wish to model, it is often useful to model an expert's posture, breathing and vocal characteristics when they are in 'expert mode'. Do they sit or stand? Do they breathe from their chest or from their stomach (diaphragm)? Do they speak quickly or slowly? And so on.

In short, effective modelling is a very precise and accurate way of carrying out the advice in the old Native American proverb: 'To really know someone you must first walk a mile in their moccasins.' Simply putting the moccasins on is not enough, you must also do the 'walking'.

Having said that, it is also important to remember that the purpose of modelling is to enable people to duplicate successful behaviour. This process is intended to assist in the transfer of skills, *not* to create clones of the expert.

20

Discipline

X, Y and NLP

According to Douglas McGregor, a professor of psychology at MIT, there are two basic styles of management.

Theory X

Managers who adopt Theory X do so on the assumption that:

- Employees are naturally lazy, irresponsible and none too bright.
- It is management's task to direct, motivate and control employees according to the needs of the organisation.

Theory Y

Managers following the Theory Y scenario assume that:

- Employees already have motivation, a readiness to accept responsibility and the potential for self-development.
- It is management's task to make it possible for people to achieve their own goals *best* by voluntarily directing their own efforts towards organisational objectives.

McGregor believed that the Theory Y assumptions encouraged positive behaviour, whilst Theory X managers were creating the very attitudes that they were complaining about. In other words, managerial style reflects managerial perceptions, and is likely to become self-fulfilling prophecy.

From George's point of view, most of his staff are reasonably good workers – as long as he keeps an eagle eye on them. The real sore thumb is Mike, highly intelligent, good at his job, but (in George's opinion) totally lacking in social skills. Whenever there is trouble about, George takes it for granted that Mike will be involved somehow.

As George has told his wife (several times), you can dream up all the theories you like, but at the end of the day the only way to deal with a person like Mike is to keep on top of him every moment of the day.

But is that really the best way to deal with 'difficult people'?

Problems and outcomes

NLP offers three vital observations which should be the foundation of every manager's portfolio of 'people skills':

■ People will always do the best they can with the resources available to them.
■ Every behaviour has a positive intention behind it.
■ Every behaviour is valid in some context.

A company (or section, or department) where it is 'safe to make mistakes' is likely to foster greater employee loyalty, greater creativity and greater commercial success. Companies which run 'by the book', on the other hand, tend to be low in rapport, low in creativity and ultimately low in profitability.

So how can these presuppositions be put into practice?

Looking for problems

The 'traditional', 'tough', 'firm', 'no nonsense' style of management tackles 'problem' situations quite confrontationally by asking some version of the following five questions:

1. What is the problem?
2. How long has it been going on?
3. Whose fault is it?
4. Why hasn't someone done something about it?
5. Who is to blame (for not sorting it out)?

In the current example, this approach will surely indicate that Mike is at fault and George had better do something about it.

Now George can give Mike a good dressing down. But does this bring them any closer to a solution?

Outcomes that work

So far, not very good.

Maybe it's time to switch to Theory Y tactics? Unfortunately, as any experienced manager knows, there are some people who don't seem to respond to the Theory Y approach either.

NLP offers a third option based on studying the required outcome rather than simply restating the problem. This process starts with a very different set of questions:

1. What do you want?
2. What will be different when you have the desired result? (What will you see, hear and feel that will let you know that things have changed?)
3. What resources are already available to you which will help you to achieve the result you desire?
4. What other resources can you draw on?
5. What is the next step?

This new way of viewing the situation shifts from generalities to specifics, and from finding problems to finding answers:

1. Determine a suitable outcome (eg a smoothly running section with everyone getting on together).
2. Describe how things will be when the situation is resolved (a solution *does* exist and *will* be implemented).
3. When we accept that Mike is doing the best he can with the resources available to him then the first step is to find out what the situation looks like to Mike. Maybe he knows there is a problem and would jump at the chance of some help. On the other hand he may think that everyone else is at fault. Either way, it would be a good idea to find out what resources Mike himself can bring to the situation. (Assigning blame is as irrelevant to good management as finding fault. Does George want to find a solution – or simply make Mike's life uncomfortable?)
4. Depending on Mike's attitude, this step involves deciding what outside resources are needed, and who is going to provide them (Mike, the company or both)?
5. Finally, what are George and Mike actually going to do? (It is important that they arrive at a solution and start to implement it as soon as is reasonably possible.)

Looking for outcomes usually means talking things through and giving guidance. Not many managers have any training in this area, and the whole process will undoubtedly take up more time and thought, as against simply making threatening noises. Still, it is a far more practical way of achieving effective solutions.

The alternative is well illustrated by an incident where a young woman had been accused of acting in a disruptive manner at work. The disciplinary procedure for this case involved six interviews, five managers and over 40 man hours. Yet when the young woman wrote a letter to each manager involved, outlining ways in which she believed she could improve her social skills, only one person replied – three weeks later.

Would you estimate that the culture in that company is geared towards finding solutions, or towards finding problems (remembering that we usually find what we expect to find)?

Hidden commands

The phenomenon of inadvertent hypnosis, or subliminal commands (Chapter 10), is particularly relevant to the disciplinary procedure. Consider the following example:

> After being reprimanded over some matter, an employee was told by their manager: 'And if anything like this happens again it will be regarded as very serious indeed.'

This typical warning seems straightforward enough, yet it actually includes some very negative hidden messages:

▨ 'Since I'm issuing this warning about the next time, I clearly don't trust you to learn from this experience' (an implicit judgement – manager to employee).
▨ 'I must keep watch on this person because I expect them to offend again' (the manager is effectively programming his future view of the employee).
▨ 'Live up to my expectations – go and re-offend' (because this manager functions by giving orders, the warning becomes an implied command – manager to employee).

These messages have added power because they are effectively 'subliminal' (insinuated but not overtly stated) and therefore do not allow for an open discussion of their validity.

The fear of falling

It might be noted here that bullying, in whatever form, also has a subliminal foundation. That is to say, bullying invariably grows out of the bully's (unconscious and unadmitted) feelings of inadequacy and a fear of losing control rather than a direct wish to inflict pain and suffering on the person being bullied.

Employers who encourage a 'macho' culture, or are inclined to tolerate bullying – including overly severe and inflexible disciplinary procedures – may want to consider the negative consequences of such a culture on employee performance:

▓ Employees revert to 'tried and trusted' patterns of behaviour (bad for creativity and ability to handle change).
▓ Employees find it difficult to recognise underlying relationships and patterns in the work environment (bad for maintaining coherent activities).
▓ Employees show reduced powers of memory and 'higher order' thinking skills (bad for company performance).
▓ Employees tend to overreact to events in the workplace (bad for employee/employee, employee/customer and employee/management relationships).

In short, bullying is not only morally unacceptable; in the long term it can become a very real threat to a company's ability to survive.

21

Appraisals

What's the point?

It might seem obvious that the yearly or half-yearly round of appraisal interviews best serves the needs of company and employees alike when the result is a more highly motivated workforce with a clear notion of how each person will raise their level of achievement in the year to come.

So isn't it strange that in so many companies the appraisal interview is surrounded by FUD – Fear, Uncertainty and Doubt!

> In an effective appraisal procedure, *both* parties are left with the sense that they have achieved a win/win result.

A key factor will be the ability of the appraiser to frame a clear outcome (Chapter 6), in which performance is measured against clearly defined, *mutually understood* expectations.

Perceptions and expectations

There is a famous experiment involving schoolteachers which shows very clearly how outcomes are moulded by our perceptions and our expectations (Chapter 3).

The teachers are told that a group of new students are either very eager and smart, or lazy and not very bright. In reality the students are selected so that the two groups are evenly matched, and about average in both attitude and ability.

As you may have guessed, the teacher who has been told that they are dealing with above average students, reports that their group are good workers and above average achievers. The teacher who thinks they are dealing with a group of problem students, however, finds that the students' behaviour, both personal and academic, is significantly below average.

What is not so easy to anticipate is the fact that many of the allegedly above average students actually do begin to achieve above average results, whilst some of the so-called underachievers begin to slip below their normal level of performance.

> If you look for people's faults then, since none of us is perfect, you will certainly find much to criticise.
>
> If you look for the good in people then, since we generally strive to do the best we know how, with the resources available to us, you will certainly find much to praise.

Onwards and upwards

As we've already said, an effective appraisal process must be based on positive, clearly defined, appropriate outcomes, having the intention of moving things 'onwards and upwards' rather than dwelling on the past.

Echoing a point made in the last chapter, three principles apply to all human behaviour:

1. Every action has a positive intention behind it.
2. Everyone has all the resources they need.
3. People can only (consciously) use the resources they know that they have, and which they know how to use.

If we expand on these basic themes:

■ People in a psychologically sound state of mind seldom if ever deliberately set out to fail or cause trouble. So reviewing the past year to pick over the mistakes, and, worse yet, offering criticism without also providing concrete suggestions for improvement is, at best, pointless.

The most realistic response to unwanted behaviour is to look for the good intention – and show the person how to achieve that intention in a more effective manner by helping them to become aware of a wider range of options.

■ A manager's job is to manage, ensuring that their subordinates have whatever resources they need to do their jobs. The difference between a poor manager and a good manager is often as simple as the difference between:

a. assuming that people '*should* know better', and
b. helping each employee in whatever way is necessary for their success.

It is interesting that some companies are now using staff appraisals as a way of assessing managerial performance.

■ Having a resource, knowing that you have that resource, and knowing how to use that resource can be three quite separate conditions. An effective appraisal will include:

- determining what resources an employee needs to fulfil their assignments, plus any resources they would like to possess (more or less relevant to their work[1]);
- identifying those resources which the employee does not consciously possess;
- drawing up a plan that will allow the employees to 'acquire' the additional resources, including on-the-job experience, formal training, self-managed learning, etc.

In short, the simple truth is that people succeed best when they are helped, encouraged and, above all, *allowed* to succeed.

---

1 Various studies have shown that employee performance tends to be enhanced by learning in general – not only by the study of topics directly related to the company's main business.

22

Negotiations

Straight down the middle

A negotiation can be as immense in its purpose as a peace treaty between two nations, or as minor as discussing whether your child can have extra pocket money.

As long as the people on one side of the deal want something from the people on the other side of the deal, and both sides are willing to discuss the issues with the intention of reaching an agreement, then you have the basis for negotiation.

The negotiating process can be broken down into just five basic steps, which can be memorised using the mnemonic **PENCE**:

> Preparation
> Estimation
> Negotiation
> Consummation
> Evaluation

In other words, any serious negotiator will start by:

- preparing his own position (step 1); and
- estimating the most likely position of the other party (step 2).

These preparatory steps are followed by the actual negotiations (step 3), the decision either to reach an agreement or to agree to abandon the negotiation process (step 4), and the post-negotiation evaluation stage (step 5).

The preparation

The foundation of any good negotiating strategy is to have an unclouded view of your own outcome(s). Not just 'I want…', but clear definitions of:

1. your ideal outcome;
2. the outcome that you expect to arrive at (approximately);
3. the least satisfactory result that you are prepared to accept.

You may, in fact, draw up several different versions of step 3, in order of acceptability. These positions are often referred to as BATNAs (*best alternative to a negotiated agreement*, or *best alternative to non-agreement*).

The other man's shoes

It is also useful to get some idea of the position(s) the other party is likely to adopt. If you are dealing with a team you have faced before then this stage should be relatively easy. If they are complete unknowns, however, it can pay dividends to brainstorm the positions they *might* take, and work out your responses.

In both cases, however, you must bear in mind that you can never be entirely sure what someone is going to do until after they've done it. Whatever guesses you come up with, be prepared to throw every single one overboard, if necessary, once the negotiations start. This is a critical situation in which to exercise the presupposition that the person (or group) with the greatest number of choices will be most likely to achieve a satisfactory outcome.

How to cut a dovetail

The most successful negotiations are those where the two sides work together to reach a mutually acceptable outcome (a 'win/win' result).

To reach such a result you will need to establish good rapport (Chapters 7 to 9), and then introduce the notion of working as a partnership rather than staging a war of attrition. It may be a novel idea to some people, but if you have indeed established rapport then it should prove acceptable.

This 'dovetailing of outcomes' is made possible when both parties reach agreement on a point of common interest as the basis for the negotiations. It may be necessary to chunk up and down (Chapter 13) from your opening positions in order to find this common point, but it will be worth the time and effort in terms of reducing the number of red herrings and hidden agendas that pop up during the rest of the negotiating process.

Whilst sharing a common outcome can help negotiations along, do remember how fallible the human memory can be. In other words: work together, emphasise areas of agreement whenever they arise, and make sure that every point agreed on verbally is fully documented and signed. Do this as you go along, before people have had time to forget exactly what has been said.

Congruency and other ways to make a point

Staying congruent (Chapter 16) during the negotiating process is a very necessary skill. Well-constructed negotiating teams invariably include someone who operates in 'Differences' mode (Chapter 12) who will be particularly aware of any incongruence in both your team and in individual team members.

When you want to 'sell' a point, especially if you expect a certain amount of resistance, always state the reasons first and then follow up with the proposal. If you put the proposal first people won't hear your justification because they'll be too busy running through all the objections they can think up.

Metaphors

As described in Chapter 15, metaphors are an excellent way of getting your message across in a non-confrontational manner. They are also something to be regarded with the deepest suspicion when you are on the receiving end!

So how might you use metaphors in a negotiating situation?

As a simple example, they can be used to indicate your own ideas about how the negotiating process should proceed:

> We had a situation like this not long ago, and the customer suggested that we do x, y and z, and sure enough we got the whole deal sewn up in next to no time. And everyone was totally satisfied with the result.

or to reject a proposal without making it personal:

> That reminds me of something I heard of just the other day. Someone over at ABC Ltd was telling me how one of their customers made a proposal much like the one you just put forward. The guys at ABC weren't entirely convinced that it was the best solution but they figured they were bound to respect the customer's decision. Come to think of it, Jerry was saying that it all ended in tears. Had to do the whole thing over from scratch. Still, that's life, I guess.

Notice that the positive stories are always about what 'we did', and the negative stories are always about someone else. This way you can give 'advice' without seeming to be saying '*we* knew best, but *they* wouldn't listen', and you and/or your company appear to be the epitome of reasonable co-operation.

Specify to clarify

Just how often do we send or receive generalised statements as though they were precise descriptions (Chapter 13)? As Kepner and Tregoe observed in their book *The Rational Manager*:

> With management growing progressively more complex, and experience more obsolete more rapidly, the manager must rely more and more on skilful, rational questioning, and less and less on experience.

This was written not, as you might imagine, in the 1980s or 1990s, but as far back as 1965. Yet it points up a problem that is as real now as it was over 40 years ago.

It's not clear whether we just don't like asking questions, so we never learn to do it well; or whether the widespread lack of effective questioning skills leads us to suppose that this does not fall within the range of learnable skills. Thus we continually fall into this kind of trap:

> **A:** 'We must have guaranteed delivery by the end of June.'
> **B:** 'No problem.'

Two months later:

> **A:** 'Your delivery was late!'
> **B:** 'No it wasn't. The goods reached you at 12.30 pm on the thirtieth of June!'
> **A:** 'That's what I mean. We said "by" the end of the month, not "at" the end of the month.'

Yet this is entirely unnecessary. There is a simple, three-step approach to questioning that allows us to be precise and accurate without resorting to something akin to interrogation:

1. Spot when details are missing.
2. Differentiate between essential and non-essential details.
3. Ask the right questions the right way to uncover the missing details (see the meta model questions in Chapter 14).

And a few points to remember when asking questions:

■ Generally speaking it is wise to avoid questions that start with 'Why?' as they will inevitably sound challenging or confrontational. (This is not an absolute rule.)

■ As regards 'open' and 'closed' questions, research shows that there is, in fact, no fixed rule as to which form is most likely to get the most detailed response. Having said that, if you aren't getting the details you need there's nothing wrong with asking what lawyers would call a leading question, along the lines of: 'So, can you help me with some details here – what did you actually tell the customer?'

■ Accept the answers you get in a reasonable manner, whether you like them or not. A response like 'You did *What!?*' can cut a potentially useful session stone dead.

■ Be willing to keep asking questions until you get the answers you really need. The person answering the questions will almost certainly be as unused to giving 'rational' answers as many people are unused to asking 'rational' questions.

23

Meetings

What are we here for?

As we've seen throughout this introduction to NLP, it is relevant to every area of business activity, for the simple reason that communication, of one sort or another, is at the heart of all business activities.

It would be easy, then, to write a complete book just on the application of NLP in meetings. Unfortunately, we don't have room to do that, so this chapter will concentrate on the six major steps that comprise any meeting – always assuming that a meeting is the best way of achieving your outcome(s):

- Specify the outcome(s).
- Agree the evidence.
- Confirm the outcome(s).
- Use sensory acuity.
- Summarize important decisions.
- Agree action.

Specify the outcome(s)

Generally speaking, the agenda for a meeting indicates the topics to be discussed, but it does little or nothing to ensure the success of that meeting.

When we talk about the outcome(s) (Chapter 6) for a meeting, we're interested in what the discussion will lead to – not just where it starts out. In this way we give the meeting focus and direction, and avoid the all too common problem of entering into inevitably fruitless discussions.

Agree the evidence

There is a widely held belief that discussing what has to be done is a time-wasting exercise and the way to succeed is simply to 'get stuck in'. A number of studies have shown that this is simply not true. Indeed, it is possible to cut the total time taken to achieve a given result by as much as a third simply by discussing the task before any action is taken.

On this basis, discussing outcomes at the very start of a meeting is far from a waste of time. Likewise there is value in agreeing how you will (jointly) know when you have satisfactorily achieved those outcomes *before* you actually try to reach any agreement.

Confirm the outcome(s)

The third (and final) step in the opening of a meeting is to check that you've all caught the same bus. That is to say, you should now summarise and confirm the outcomes that have been agreed upon, and what will have to be true in order to know that those outcomes have been achieved. This will be far more successful if the items in question are written down and circulated. If they can be sent out to be printed up whilst the meeting continues, so much the better.

Use sensory acuity

Throughout the course of the meeting it is important to be alert to what is really going on (that is, be aware of what people do

– don't depend on what they say). If someone says they agree on a particular point, but shows non-verbal evidence of confusion or doubt, be sure to deal with those non-verbal cues before the meeting is over or the agreement you have reached may be short-lived.

Do remember that different people have different convincer modes (Chapter 12) – one agreement does not (necessarily) a deal make.

Summarise important decisions

Just as you established solid confirmation of the outcome(s) for the meeting, make sure that all important decisions reached in the course of the meeting are also summarised and agreed.

Summarising has the added advantage of being a good way of checking that you all agree not just on the wording but also on the meaning of each decision.

Agree action

And finally, agree on the action to be taken on the basis of the decisions that have been made. These actions should feature in the minutes when they are circulated to the participants so that everyone knows what's going on, who has responsibility for the various follow-up actions, and any disputes can be aired (and settled) as quickly as possible.

Challenge for relevance

Whenever (if ever) a meeting seems to be losing focus because someone is (in your opinion) going into too much detail, taking too broad an overview, or simply diverging from the point, be confident enough to firmly and politely challenge the speaker to explain what relevance their point has to the agreed outcome(s) for the meeting.

Having said that, do remember to challenge the point, not the person making the point. The aim is to keep the meeting on track, not to create friction. Remember, every action has a positive intention, and even the most irritating nit-picker may have a valid point to make.

24

Sales

It's the way that you do it

One of the current business buzzwords is 'differentiation' – the process of making your own product or service stand out from all of its (very similar) rivals. What very few professional service businesses seem to understand is that differentiation has very little to do with the product as such. When you are competing in a market full of nearly identical products there's little mileage in stressing the negligible differences between one product and another. It is usually better to concentrate on the 'halo' around your product – the associations which will make that item or service *appear* to be more desirable.

Most people, from the loftiest CEO to the typical 'man in the street', are essentially creatures of habit. They develop certain buying patterns, which are unlikely to change without a very good reason. And the reason is likely to be personal rather than business-oriented. (In a recent study, 76 per cent of the companies that changed suppliers had done so because the relationship with the supplier's rep had broken down in some way.)

However unbusinesslike it may seem, in a selling situation developing rapport with the customer matters far more than mere technical details (Chapters 7–9).

Believe it or not, the fact that your product or service is

genuinely superior to everything else on the market is not necessarily your customer's primary concern.

To tell or not to tell

As we saw in Chapter 3, everyone has their own 'world view', which means that any person you are selling to will have their own individual set of reasons for buying – or not buying – whatever it is you are selling.

So, if you go into a selling situation and immediately start to tell the customer about your product or service (hereafter I'll use the word 'product' to refer to both) then you will be selling, at best, to some mythical 'Mr Average', or at worst, to yourself. That is to say, you will be telling the customer what you believe they *ought* to want to hear, or you will be telling them what *you* would want to hear.

In neither case are you treating the customer as a real person.

> The person asking the questions controls the conversation.

Features and benefits

In order to enter your customer's world, which is, after all, where the sale will actually take place, you must ask questions which will encourage the customer to tell you what you really need to know (known in NLP as 'eliciting the customer's buying strategy'). These questions need to be simple and precise:

'What did you like most about your last fleet car supplier?'
'Is there any way in which they could have given better service?'
'What did you least like about XYZ Training Ltd?'
'In what way did they fail to meet your training needs?'

Once you have a clear idea of what the customer actually wants from the product that you are selling, you can frame your sales pitch to show how specific 'features' of your product can *benefit* the customer by answering specific needs. Incidentally, if you can't match a particular need, or if there are features of your product which don't relate to any of the customer's declared needs, *leave that information out of your presentation*. No matter how many wonderful bells and whistles your product may have, the customer will only buy, and be satisfied with, what the *customer* actually wants.

How, then, can you help the customer to find out what they really want? This question brings us back to the subject of PTSs (Primary Thinking Styles – Chapters 5 and 17).

Selling to visual mode customers

Even when you think you know what they want, trying to *tell* a customer or client what your product can do for them, when they are in visual mode, will be a total waste of time – unless you paint 'word pictures' for them. A customer in visual mode wants to *see* what they're getting for their money, be it a car, a holiday, a new pair of shoes or a computer upgrade.

Be prepared to be patient going in to the sale – when someone is in visual mode they often want to literally *view* all the alternatives before making a final decision. Give them the time they want, and don't try to talk to them until they've reached the 'shortlist' stage, at which point you can help the process along by asking questions that stimulate visual images:

'Can you see yourself lying on that beautiful golden beach?'
'The hi-tech styling really works well on this CD player, doesn't it?'
'Just imagine the other drivers trying not to stare as you glide down the motorway in this beauty.'

When a customer in visual mode does come to a decision, they usually do so quickly and with conviction (they have finally built a mental picture which looks right). Avoid too much chit-chat. If you disturb that mental image you may literally talk yourself out of a sale.

Finally, if a customer in visual mode isn't ready to make an on-the-spot commitment, make sure you give them some kind of visual reminder to take away with them.

Selling to auditory mode customers

It might seem logical to suppose that the best way to sell to customers in auditory mode would be by talking about your product, yet in practice exactly the opposite is true. It is especially important that you give someone who is in auditory mode as much opportunity as possible to talk to you.

As soon as a person in auditory mode begins to interrupt or raise their voice you know that they have started an internal review of the sale. Listen carefully and they will tell you everything you need to know to complete a mutually satisfactory transaction – nuggets such as when they last made a similar purchase, and, even more importantly, what triggered their decision on that previous occasion.

Be prepared to answer questions, but remember that the most effective salesperson for someone in auditory mode is their own voice. If they start to repeat themselves then the sale probably isn't happening. In this case listen carefully to what they are saying (to find out where the barrier is), then reframe the barrier (Chapter 11) to allow the sale to progress.

Selling to kinaesthetic mode customers

Making a sale to a customer or client who is in kinaesthetic mode can be very easy and very difficult – and both in the same transaction.

The process is easy in so far as people in kinaesthetic mode are concerned, because they readily respond to emotionally charged presentations and to 'hands-on' experience of the product – as long as the salesperson's enthusiasm doesn't become a hustle.

The bad news is that whilst a person is in kinaesthetic mode they will tend to buy in response to their feelings, and are quite likely to change their mind about a purchase just as soon as the accompanying emotion fades away. When this happens they will not necessarily regret having bought the item (although they are the group most likely to suffer from 'buyer's remorse'). Rather they will start to question whether they got a good deal, whether the purchase was really necessary, and so on. (This indecision is even more likely if anyone questions them about their purchase.)

In order to minimise the effects of this 'aftershock' syndrome, it is necessary to provide built-in reassurance.

IBM used to have a slogan along the lines of:

No one ever got fired for buying IBM.

True or not, the effect of the slogan was to reassure people who were in kinaesthetic mode that they had made the right choice by redirecting their fears towards the possible consequences of any alternative action (ie buying from our competitors *could* seriously damage your career).

Likewise, the documentation that accompanies many electrical goods congratulating the customer on their wise choice and asking them to register for after-sales support is an excellent way of reassuring people in kinaesthetic mode, and impulse buyers that they have made the right decision.

Selling to groups

You may be thinking that this is fine for sales to individual customers, but not much use when dealing with *groups* of customers. In practice the information is equally valid in both situations. After all, a group is composed of individuals, so you still need to deal with individual PTSs. The only difference when dealing with a group is that you need to use your sensory acuity to single out the key member(s) of the group, and identify their PTS(s). Then weight your sales presentation accordingly.

Watch for the person or people who seem most at ease, who clearly are not afraid to express an opinion, who are the focus of attention for the rest of the group, and so on. If you're still not sure who the key figures (ie decision makers) are, simply tailor your presentation to cover all three PTSs more or less equally. In this manner you're bound to be on the same wavelength with everyone in the audience at some time or other. It's not very scientific, but it's better than achieving no rapport at all.

More NLP resources can be found on the author's website http://www.bradburyae.mistral.co.uk

Basic NLP terms used in this book

(Words in italics are described elsewhere in the list of terms.)

Anchor An 'anchor' is a link between an internal *state* and an external stimulus (eg a piece of music that recalls a past event).

Anchoring The process of creating an *anchor*. Anchors can be created deliberately or by chance. They can also be altered and even removed ('dissolved').

As if
1. An event can be dealt with through visualisation 'as if' it had actually happened.
2. There is proven value in adopting certain presuppositions 'as if' they were true, even though it hasn't been proved that they are universally true.

Associated To be 'associated' with a given event or memory is to view it as someone taking part in that event.
(See also *Dissociated*).

Auditory mode Using sound as the PTS
(See also *Kinaesthetic mode*, *PTS* and *Visual mode*.)

Beliefs An idea about some aspect of ourselves or the external world which we hold to be true without having any objective supporting evidence – 'I've never tried it, I just know [*believe*] I won't like it.'
(See also *Values*.)

Chunk One or more items of information which a given person can handle as a single concept or idea.

Chunking
1. Dividing a large piece of information into smaller 'chunks'.
2. Moving from details to generalities ('chunking up') or vice versa ('chunking down').

Congruence (external) External congruence exists when your body language, vocal signals and verbal message all send the same message.
Being externally congruent is closely related to your level of *internal congruence*.

Congruence (internal) Internal congruence exists when you are completely focused on the task in hand *and* you are at ease about the situation (ie when all of your 'parts' are in harmony).

Conscious That part of the mind which is immediately accessible. It is the conscious mind which can only hold seven items of information, plus or minus two.

Content In any communication, the 'content' is the message you are giving out – as distinct from other people's interpretation of your message.
(See also *Process* and *State*.)

Crossover mirroring Indirectly matching another person's body language – you scratch your neck, I rub my arm – usually as part of the process of establishing rapport.

Deletion The process of ignoring certain items of information about some event or person (for *any* reason).

Dissociated To be dissociated from an event or memory is to view it as though watching it as an observer.
(See also *Associated.*)

Distortion The process of reshaping information so that it misrepresents external reality (for *any* reason).

Dovetailing (**outcomes**) Matching your outcome with someone else so that both outcomes can be achieved as far as this is possible. Note that dovetailing implies reaching a reasonable compromise but does not require you to sacrifice your own interests in favour of the other party.

Frame The context within which a person, thing or event is *perceived.*

Generalisation The process of creating a general rule or assumption on the basis of a very limited amount of evidence.

Kinaesthetic mode Using feelings – physical and/or emotional – as the primary information processing sense.
(See also *Auditory mode*, *PTS* and *Visual mode.*)

Leading Doing something different from the person with whom you are communicating, usually after a period of *pacing.*

Matching Discreetly copying someone else's body language as part of the process of creating and maintaining *rapport* (you cross your arms – I cross my arms, etc).

Mental map In this context, a mental representation of a person, event or thing. All mental maps are, by definition, incomplete and out of date. Nevertheless, they are the best information we have about 'reality'.

Meta program An internal filter used to process incoming information and determine an appropriate reaction.

Metaphor A story – based or partly based on real or entirely fictional events – designed to convey a message so that it will be more readily received by the listener.

Mirroring Synonymous with *matching*.

Modal operators Internal rules by which people govern their own behaviour and judge the behaviour of others.

Modelling A basic NLP skill, in this context modelling is the process of capturing the thoughts and actions which distinguish an expert in some field from someone who is merely competent. The information must be described in such a way that it is possible for other people to replicate the relevant elements in order to enhance their own skill level.

Outcome (well-formed) A goal or want which has been

- consciously and specifically defined in positive terms;
- can be achieved by the individual setting the outcome with minimal external help; and
- has no discernible detrimental consequences.

Pacing *Matching* and *mirroring* another person's body language to help build rapport, often prior to *leading* (see above).

Perceptions Our conscious view of the external world. Our perceptions are often shaped by our *beliefs*, *values* and expectations.

Process In any communication, the 'process' element is the way that you handle your side of the communication.

PTS Primary (or preferred) thinking style – *Auditory*, *Kinaesthetic*, *Visual*. The sense which we use most frequently in assessing and describing the external world.

Rapport A state of mutual trust and respect existing between two or more people. Rapport is the primary basis for all successful communications.

Reality (external) The totality of the universe outside our skins. Since nothing is completely knowable our view of external reality is always limited.

Reality (internal) Internal reality is what is 'real' to a given individual – their current *mental map* of external reality.

Reframe Re-stating a view of *reality* (internal or external), usually in order to make it easier to deal with.

Resource Any internal quality (confidence, humour, calmness, etc) which makes it easier to perform a required task.
Having a resource does not necessarily mean that we know that we have it, and even when we know that we have a particular resource we may still need time and guidance to learn how to use it effectively.

Resourceful state Being aware that you have, and know how to use, the *resources* required in a given situation.

Sensory acuity The skill of being sensitive to a person's non-verbal changes (rate of speech, skin colour, muscle tension, etc), which give clues to their mental activity.

State Your actual condition (emotional, physical and mental), appropriate or otherwise, at any particular moment.

Thinking (multiple choice) Thinking based on the (usually correct) view that there are as many options as you can think of – and then some.

Thinking (two-valued) Thinking based on the (usually incorrect) assumption that there are only two options in a given situation.

Ultradian rhythm A naturally occurring pattern of alternating consciousness, consisting of approximately 90 minutes of normal awareness followed by about 20 minutes of semi-trance-like consciousness. The rhythm continues throughout both day and night, except that at night the 90 minute periods are spent in normal sleep, whilst the 20 minute periods are generally when REM (rapid eye movement) sleep and dreaming take place.

Unconscious The part of your mind which you are usually not aware of. The unconscious mind can handle vast amounts of information and multiple activities simultaneously.

Values Filters we use to evaluate incoming messages about ourselves and the world around us – good/bad, worthwhile/worthless, and so on. Our values are normally closely tied to our *beliefs*.

Visual mode Using sight as the primary information processing sense.
(See also *Auditory mode, PTS and Kinaesthetic mode.*)

The new *Creating Success* series

Published in association with

0 7494 4751 6   Paperback   2006

0 7494 4558 0   Paperback   2006

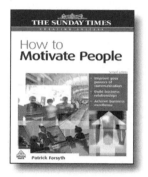

0 7494 4551 3   Paperback   2006

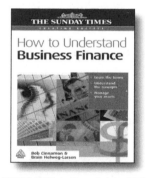

0 7494 4668 4   Paperback   2006

0 7494 4553 X   Paperback   2006

0 7494 4554 8   Paperback   2006

The new *Creating Success* series

Published in association with

0 7494 4552 1   Paperback   2006

0 7494 4550 5   Paperback   2006

0 7494 4560 2   Paperback   2006

0 7494 4561 0   Paperback   2006

0 7494 4559 9   Paperback   2006

0 7494 4665 X   Paperback   2006

For further information on how to order, please visit

www.kogan-page.co.uk

Other titles in the Kogan Page Creating Success series

The above titles are available from all good bookshops. For further information on these and other Kogan Page titles, or to order online, visit the Kogan Page website at **www.kogan-page.co.uk**